I LIE
FOR A
LIVING

INTERNATIONAL SPY MUSEUM

Greatest Spies
of All Time

ANTONY SHUGAAR

Foreword by PETER EARNEST,
Executive Director of the International Spy Museum
Illustrations by Steven Guarnaccia

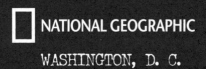

NATIONAL GEOGRAPHIC

WASHINGTON, D. C.

Founded in 1888, the National Geographic Society is one of the largest nonprofit scientific and educational organizations in the world. It reaches more than 285 million people worldwide each month through its official journal, NATIONAL GEOGRAPHIC, and its four other magazines; the National Geographic Channel; television documentaries; radio programs; films; books; videos and DVDs; maps; and interactive media. National Geographic has funded more than 8,000 scientific research projects and supports an education program combating geographic illiteracy.

For more information, please call 1-800-NGS LINE (647-5463)
or write to the following address:

National Geographic Society, 1145 17th Street N.W.,
Washington, D.C. 20036-4688 U.S.A.

Log on to nationalgeographic.com; AOL Keyword: NatGeo.

"WHY'D HE DO IT?"

That's the man in the street's first question when confronted with a headline exposé of a major spy. In
America, from Maj. Gen. Benedict Arnold right down
to senior FBI career counterintelligence agent Robert
Hanssen: "Why?" It's treason. Selling out your country.
From the dawn of history, branded one of mankind's most
despicable crimes. Every time you see Hanssen's beaming
countenance grinning out at you from the newsstand, you
feel it personally: He's rubbing salt in your wounds.

But that's the man in the street's reaction. What about
the professional intelligence and counterintelligence
officers, the ones who recruit spies for a living or catch
them? When a spy case breaks, what do the pros want to
know? You'd be surprised. It's usually not, "Why'd he do
it?" but, "How'd he do it?" and "What'd he get (the 'take')?"
In other words, the pros want to learn the spy's "methods"
(as in "sources and methods") and his degree of success.

Now you, the reader, have a chance to scan a whole
bunch of real spy cases at a sitting--maybe not all, but
many. This is what the pros do. They're no longer shocked

or even surprised at the richness and diversity of spying through history or at the incredibly broad range of motivations that lead individuals to that life-endangering extreme.

As a case officer in the Clandestine Service of the Central Intelligence Agency (CIA) for some 25 years, I was deeply immersed in the world of assessing, recruiting, and acquiring new assets (agents) locally and in the Soviet/East European arena. Assessing prospective recruitment subjects (targets) and their apparent motivations consumed my days. And remember, ones understanding of another's motivation is "through a glass darkly" at best and often quite distorted--even to the individual himself.

Now you're looking at spies whose motivations still merit study, but they're no longer spies; they've been caught, exposed, have surfaced, confessed, and even written their memoirs. You can focus not only on why but how they did what they say they did--their methods--and how well (success). Look for patterns. Look for the absence of patterns and the similarity of rationales for their actions. Look for models to compare with some of the figures in your everyday lives. These are not stick figures but flesh and blood examples of real individuals who chose to take another path--some for the basest of reasons, and some for the noblest.

PETER EARNEST
Executive Director of the International Spy Museum

THE ANCIENT ART OF SPYING

The history, or perhaps the tradition, of spying runs deep. Whatever the historical accuracy of the Bible, the archetypes are there. Lucifer, once an angel, became the first rogue recruit to the Other Side (and in fact, the term "Main Adversary" is both KGB parlance and, literally, Scripture), the first agent to go officially "off the reservation." He quickly mobilized his forces, sending the dangerously persuasive Serpent into the Garden of Eden: the first agent of influence.

And indeed the earliest history of intelligence and espionage is pretty much the history of human nature. Covert action is a technical term; sneaking around, stealing things, and killing people are instinctive acts, performed for elementary reasons.

In the history of spying, however, things become more interesting when these instinctive actions become institutionalized. Historian Rose Mary Sheldon recently described spying in antiquity in an essay entitled "Toga and Dagger." The frustrations and snafus of intelligence were common then as well: Julius Caesar was reportedly holding a list of conspirators in his hand as he was assassinated, and had not yet had time to scan the names. Perhaps, in response to Caesar's dismayed exclamation of "Et tu, Brute?" Brutus may have snarled under his breath, as he closed in for the fatal blow, "Read the report."

The Romans had learned from the best: Hannibal of Carthage not only used weapons of mass destruction (elephants) in his war on the Romans, he had a network of spies that infiltrated Roman camps and used secret hand signals to identify themselves to one another. And Hannibal was a stern spymaster. When one of his scouts provided bad intelligence, sending the Carthaginian army into an ambush, the scout was crucified. Literally.

The intelligence game was different in the ancient world, but perhaps not all that different. They had no spy satellites, no predator drones, but there was stealth and sudden destruction. The Greek scientist Archimedes, who lived about the same time as Hannibal, was working for Hiero II, tyrant of the Sicilian city-state of Syracuse, when the Roman fleet laid siege. Archimedes set up and focused an array of highly polished mirrors on the fleet--which had anchored just outside the range of arrow-shot--and set them aflame from that distance. Shades of Star Wars!

This digression into some of the technologies of the ancient world (there were many others, including primitive steam engines, cog-and-gear computers, and hydraulic organs, which apparently provided the soundtrack for gladiatorial matches) helps to illustrate that ancient espionage was surely as sophisticated and devious as anything we have today.

One documented method of steganography, or secret writing, involved shaving the head of a messenger, tattooing the message onto his skin, and allowing the hair to grow back. Effective, but time-consuming. Though documentation of a quicker, less expensive method (requiring the use of one egg per message, instead of one living messenger) dates back only to the Renaissance, the ancients may also have used it. By writing on the shell of a hard-boiled egg, it was possible to create a message on the white of the egg within, without leaving a trace on the shell itself. The recipient would crack open the shell to read the concealed message.

In the ancient world, the names used for spies varied, and were often as bland and anonymous as the persona of the perfect spy. One name from the Roman Empire was *frumentarii*, or grain inspectors, since those officers were often used as secret agents. And in fact, the very term "secret agent" derives from the title that replaced frumentarii, the imperial *agentes in rebus*, or operatives in matters, a safely generic term. Other terms included the Greek equivalents *kataskopoi* and *kryptei*, the Latin *speculatores*, and last of all, the senior officers overseeing the agentes in rebus, the *curiosi*. To our ears it sounds like they were prying, but in Latin curiosi probably sounded more like those who were careful or cautious.

There was espionage aplenty in the years that followed, leading up to the creation of modern intelligence establishments in the 16th century. The Mongols had outstanding networks of spies, scouts, and informers. A great German banking house, the Fugger family, received reports from their envoys on matters ranging from the trivial (the birth of a three-headed calf, for instance) to the monumental (the progress and destruction of the Spanish Armada). This story is continued in the spy biographies that follow.

It was not until the turn of the 20th century that our present-day understanding of spies appeared in the legal code, with the 1911 passage of Britain's Official Secrets Act. The shift from the idea of a spy as something like a secretive military scout in wartime to the modern concept of a secret agent is also reflected in the entry for "Spy" in the 1911 Encyclopaedia Britannica. The article is in two parts: The first section, signed by the author, defines a spy as "in war—a person who, disguised or without bearing the distinguishing marks of belligerent forces, mixes with the enemy for the purpose of obtaining information useful to the army he is serving." In a second section, clearly added in a nod to the changing definition of the term, "the term 'spy' is applied also to those who in time of peace secretly endeavour to obtain information concerning the forces, armaments, fortifications or defences of a country for the purpose of supplying it to another country." Prudish, stilted, impossibly quaint—and yet this marks the advent of the modern idea of spying. The article goes on to note that "most countries have legislation dealing with 'spying' in time of peace." Most of that legislation was recent, dating back only a decade or two.

To conclude this brief historical overview, consider the statue of Nathan Hale that stands outside CIA headquarters. Some have called its presence ironic: He was caught and hanged at the very beginning of his career. Some feel that his last words might just as well have been, "I have not yet begun to spy," instead of the line about regretting only having one life to lose for his country. But perhaps, if there is irony here, a canny CIA insider would point out that it is not the obvious surface layer of irony that the "Company" boasts a statue to a blundering spy. The spies that are known to the public, the insider might say, are the spies that get caught. The spies who live to a comfortable, anonymous old age will do just fine without a statue, thank you very much. And without a recognized place in history.

SPYMASTERS

PULLING THE PUPPET STRINGS

ladimiro Montesinos, Peru's former spymaster and the man who dismantled the Shining Path guerrilla movement, is now an occupant of a prison he built. His cell neighbors include the leader of Shining Path, Abimael Guzman. In a bizarre twist of history, the spymaster and the terrorist leader that the spymaster caught are fellow prisoners of a democratic system of justice.

Some spymasters, such as Cardinal Richelieu, George Washington, William Donovan, and Allen Dulles, die prosperous and respected. Walsingham, Elizabeth I's spymaster, certainly outlived Mary Queen of Scots (indeed, he engineered her execution), though he died three years before his former agent Christopher Marlowe (who may have been murdered by another of Walsingham's former agents). But at the end of his life he was relegated to the periphery of power and was eking out an existence on a meager pension.

Oddly, Markus Wolf, the former head of the foreign intelligence branch of East Germany's Stasi, is retired comfortably, living in part off the proceeds of a film deal he made with a Hollywood producer.

FRANCIS WALSINGHAM

SPYMASTER FOR ELIZABETH I

Sir Francis Walsingham created one of the first modern intelligence services in a situation remarkably similar to the Cold War. The "world" (at the time, western Europe) was split into two ideological blocs: Catholicism and Protestantism. It was a time when the term "popish" was bandied about in England as "Commie" was here in the fifties.

As secretary of state of England under Elizabeth I, Walsingham established a network of spies in some of the critical points of a divided Christendom, paying many of them out of his own pocket (in fact, he died penniless as a result). He is even thought to have recruited the playwright Christopher Marlowe as an agent, though little is known about the work Marlowe did during his many trips to the Continent. It is known that when Marlowe was failing his coursework at Cambridge, the Queen's privy council interceded on his behalf.

To carry the analogy to the Cold War a little further, Walsingham was ambassador to France during the arguable equivalent of the Hungarian uprising of 1956: the Saint Bartholomew's Day massacre of 1572. He sheltered Huguenots—outlawed French Protestants—in his own home, and came close to being killed himself, returning to England badly shaken.

Later in his career, he managed the investigation and prosecution of the Babington Plot to murder Queen Elizabeth. He personally persuaded the queen that the evidence warranted the execution of her own cousin and rival to the throne, Mary, Queen of Scots.

That was just a year before the attack of the Spanish Armada. A recently unearthed document suggests that Walsingham actually came to terms of some sort in the mid-1580s with the powerful

A true believer in Protestantism, and in queen and country, Walsingham created the first modern intelligence system for Elizabeth I.

Ottoman Porte (court) to encourage the Turks to harass Spanish shipping in the Mediterranean. There is reason to think that by the time the Armada attacked in 1588, Spanish seapower had been weakened by this distracting and artfully stage-managed sideshow.

Throughout his career, Walsingham was a valuable watchdog, thwarting numerous attempts on the Virgin Queen's life and pushing constantly for an attack on England's great maritime rival, Spain. Walsingham was that most dangerous kind of spymaster: a true believer (in Protestantism, and in queen and country). His relentless insistence on attack and confrontation undercut his role as an adviser with Elizabeth, who was stingy with money (of which she always had too little) and always keen to delay battle until her military forces could grow. And so, if Walsingham had a defect as the chief of the forerunner of England's intelligence service, it was that he was a little too hot-blooded for the Cold War of that time.

CARDINAL RICHELIEU
THE RED EMINENCE

Richelieu's far-reaching spy ring supplied a steady stream of information that transformed France into a great power.

The life of Cardinal Armand Jean du Plessis de Richelieu was rich in dramatic moments, but few of them could equal the stark tension of November 10, 1630. Louis XIII had become king of France as a boy, when his father was assassinated; his reign had been dominated by the personality of the queen mother, Marie de Médicis, who continued to rule for several years after her term as regent officially expired. Mediating between the two was Richelieu, upon whom the weak and mentally unstable king, now in his late-20s, relied.

The queen mother had persuaded the king to dismiss Richelieu, dubbed the Red Eminence for his immense influence; the king had come to his mother's apartment in the Luxembourg Palace for a final talk. Orders had been given that they were not to be disturbed on any account, but as the king and the Italian-born queen mother debated Richelieu's fate, the thin, goateed Cardinal stepped into the room from the unguarded chapel door.

Marie de Médicis had seen a great deal in her life, but this bold and stealthy move left her speechless for a moment. As soon as she gathered her wits, however, she burst into a stream of invective. Richelieu left the room, sure that his daring move had sealed his doom. Instead, in what was known as the Day of the Dupes, Richelieu kept his hold on power, and the queen mother eventually fled France.

In an 18-year career that shaped France and Europe, Richelieu focused ruthlessly on consolidating the French king's absolute power and undermining the ancient imperial power of the Habsburg dynasty. He did so through intrigue, intimidation, and, especially, intelligence. His network of spies spanned the globe (many French missionaries reported back to him), focusing on the Habsburg capital of Vienna. Indeed, it has been observed that Vienna's history as a shadowy capital of espionage began with Richelieu's spy ring.

His efforts were successful: France became a great power, and it can safely be said that Richelieu laid the foundations for the splendid reign of the king that succeeded his own, Louis XIV, whose rule ultimately led to the end of the Holy Roman Empire.

Some of his alliances were misguided. In a diplomatic move comparable to Nixon's trip to China, the Roman Catholic prelate encouraged Gustave Adolphus of Sweden, a Protestant king, to invade Germany, with unfortunate results: the Thirty Years War.

But Richelieu's authority, based on both his grim personality and his ubiquitous spies, never wavered. One of his last acts was to sail up the Rhone in his stately barge with De Thou, one of the conspirators of the Cinq Mars plot to betray France, bound securely in a small boat trailing behind, to Lyons. There De Thou was tried and executed.

GEORGE WASHINGTON
REVOLUTIONARY SPYMASTER

George Washington famously said, "I cannot tell a lie." He might have added, "I have people who do that for me."

And the British realized that—to their enormous chagrin. Maj. George Beckwith, chief of British intelligence in the Colonies at the culmination of the Revolutionary War, had the highest regard for Washington as a spymaster. "Washington did not really outfight the British, he simply outspied us!" Beckwith said.

Washington learned the value of intelligence early. He was just 21, a very young major in the British army, when he was sent west to deliver an ultimatum to the French, in the lead-up to the last of the French and Indian wars. He trekked through winter snow almost all the way to Lake Erie, spending 78 days in the wilderness. During his journey he learned the location of the French forts and the broad out-lines of their war plans from a group of drunken French soldiers. He also observed a small fleet of French war canoes.

His return home was fraught with dangers—he nearly drowned in an ice-choked river, and an Indian he met in the woods shot at him from very close range, and missed—but the intelligence he carried back won him renown and praise.

Just a few years later, he was appointed colonel and made com-mander-in-chief of all Virginia forces; at age 23, he was expected to defend 300 miles of mountainous frontier with about 300 men, a job for which intelligence reports must have been crucial.

These were his early years; when he again served in a position of military responsibility, he was rapidly catapulted to supreme com-mand. He immediately made use of spies, and in time he developed

Washington understood very early in his career the value of sound intelligence.

complex networks of spies engaged in counterintelligence operations, and even established deception schemes as sophisticated as those used to fool the Germans prior to D-Day. Before the Battle of Yorktown, Washington collected boats on the New Jersey shore to convince the British he was preparing an invasion of Manhattan island; he set up a large camp in Chatham, N.J., and even established a bakery that could feed an army.

And just a few days before Christmas, 1776, Washington staged a scuffle and the subsequent arrest of one of his agents, a meat merchant named Honeyman who had been supplying the British army of Hessian troops across the Delaware River. Imprisoned as a spy, Honeyman escaped after a haystack "somehow" caught fire. He made his way through British lines, and allayed British fears of an American attack—which, of course, came the day after Christmas, and resulted in an overwhelming triumph for the demoralized American troops.

Throughout the Revolutionary War, one of Washington's most important spy networks was in the British-held New York City area. The nucleus of that network was the Culper Ring.

The workings of the Culper Ring were sophisticated and interesting. Documents, written in code and in a special invisible ink—developed for him by Sir James Jay, the brother of John Jay, who would later become the first chief justice of the Supreme Court—were conveyed from the chief agent in Manhattan, Robert Townsend, known in code as Culper Jr., by a tavernkeeper who regularly traveled to Long Island for supplies. There they were placed in a dead drop—that is, placed in a box and buried—on the farm of the second agent, Abraham Woodhull, known as Culper Sr. The next step was particularly intricate. A neighbor, Anna Smith Strong, would signal to Culper Sr. through a system involving washing hanging on a line. When a sailor named Caleb Brewster was waiting to pick up the message from Culper Sr., Mrs. Strong would hang a black petticoat and a certain number of white handkerchiefs out to dry. The number of handkerchiefs would direct Culper Sr. to one of six coves, where the document would be sent on its way across Long Island Sound and, from there, by mounted courier to General Washington's office.

Laundry figured in another of Washington's intelligence coups: When Sir Henry Clinton, the new commander of British forces stationed in Philadelphia, learned that French troops were landing in America, he decided to pull his forces back quickly to New York. A sudden rush of orders to the city's laundries ensued, and several agents who worked as washerwomen reported the flurry back to Washington (a similar flurry of pizza orders was apparently placed in the area around the Pentagon on the evening before the ground war began in Iraq in 1991).

One of Washington's agents was Lydia Darragh, an Irishwoman and Quaker living in Philadelphia. British troops had requisitioned her house, but she managed to talk them into letting her stay in the house with her two young children. The parlor was used by British officers for staff meetings, and apparently as Lydia eavesdropped, she succeeded in actually overhearing the order for British troops to march at dawn in a surprise attack.

Lydia's husband then encoded the information on small pieces of paper that Lydia sewed into cloth-covered buttons, which she then stitched onto the coat of her teenage son, who then went to see his brother, Charles Darragh, a lieutenant in Washington's army.

One of the officers involved in the meeting was Maj. John André, who was later hanged as a British spy. He knocked on Lydia's door after the meeting to see if she had been eavesdropping. He was not much of a counterintelligence officer however: She pretended to be sleepy, and that was enough to fool him.

ALLAN PINKERTON
UNION SPYMASTER

Pinkerton's agents caught several important Confederate spies, including Belle Boyd, whom they released.

On April 19, 1865, Allan Pinkerton wrote from New Orleans to the secretary of war: "This morning's papers contain the deplorable intelligence of the assassination of President Lincoln and Secretary Seward.... In 1861, I was enabled to save him from the fate he has now met. How I regret that I had not been near him previous to this fatal act. I might have been the means to arrest it." The letter was signed: E. J. Allen.

Pinkerton was referring to a plot to kill the President-elect that he had uncovered while working as a railroad detective, investigating threatened sabotage against the railroads. He learned that several well-born young men of Baltimore (and an Italian barber!) hoped to kill Lincoln before he could be sworn in. Pinkerton urged Lincoln to pass through Baltimore stealthily, by night (wearing a cape and a tam-o'-shanter), and his advice was taken.

The message was vintage Pinkerton: slightly self-aggrandizing, and accurate in some details, not in others (Seward was wounded, not killed). The pseudonymous signature refers to the war years that followed. As a result of Pinkerton's timely (and, according to Lincoln's bodyguard, completely fictitious) warning, Gen. George McClellan hired him to organize "a secret service force" under the alias of E. J. Allen. Allen was "continually occupied in procuring from all possible sources information regarding the strength, positions, and movements of the enemy," according to McClellan.

Despite his qualifications—founder of one of the largest private detective agencies in the country, and a former "stationmaster" on the Underground Railroad—Pinkerton, unfortunately, got his facts wrong on more than one occasion. He told McClellan that Lee had 200,000 men, when in fact he had fewer than half that number. Pinkerton's exaggerated numbers kept McClellan from pressing his huge advantage at Antietam. Ultimately, Lincoln fired McClellan, saying he had a "bad case of the slows," and the general then ran for President against Lincoln in 1864.

Despite this unfortunate set of results, Pinkerton and his men went on to catch several Confederate spies. But Pinkerton personally interrogated Belle Boyd and decided to let her go.

One of his most successful operations during the Civil War involved the debriefing of escaped slaves; he also used them as agents, and their reports were known as Black Dispatches.

McClellan's firing in late 1862 marked the end of Pinkerton's "secret service force." A few years later, one of his detectives infiltrated the Molly Maguires, a secret association of coal miners accused of anti-mine-owner terrorism. The detective went undercover and helped to break up the ring. The Pinkertons claimed this was anti-terrorism; others saw it as strikebreaking.

WILLIAM DONOVAN

DIRECTOR OF THE OSS

It never seemed that William J. Donovan sought his role as the head of the Office of Strategic Services; if anything, the OSS came looking for him. He was a well-connected millionaire lawyer, one of the most highly decorated soldiers in World War I (including the Medal of Honor), had lost an election for governor of New York, and had briefly supervised a young J. Edgar Hoover. He had served in combat against Pancho Villa and helped Herbert Hoover organize famine relief in war-torn Europe. For fun, he visited the war zones of Italian-occupied Ethiopia and civil war Spain. A friend once commented that the poet e. e. cummings might have been thinking of Donovan when he wrote "And how do you like your blue-eyed boy, Mr. Death?"

In contrast to this sparkling resumé, America's intelligence service in 1940 was, in the words of one senior diplomat, "primitive and inadequate...timid, parochial, and operating strictly in the tradition of the Spanish-American War."

That changed once FDR assigned "Wild" Bill (though some called him "Hush Hush" Bill) to become coordinator of information and, in time, director of the OSS. As befit his understanding of the many-faceted aspects of intelligence, he began by mining existing sources of information, enlisting the support of the Librarian of Congress (poet Archibald MacLeish) for the work of his Research and Analysis Branch. A crew of nearly a thousand top scholars, including a couple of Nobel laureates, identified targets for U.S. bombers: first the fighter aircraft factories, then oil fields, and finally, the synthetic fuel plants the Nazis were using to make up for lost oil production.

"Wild" Bill Donovan was also known as "Hush Hush" Bill for his OSS work.

At its height, the OSS employed about 13,000 men and women, and over its four-year existence spent 135 million dollars.

The work of the OSS was hardly limited to research. It ran the three-man "Jedburgh" teams (named after the Scottish city where Allied agents trained for intelligence and sabotage missions) that parachuted into occupied France just before the Normandy invasion, it ran an army in Burma of nearly 11,000 native Kachins to fight the occupying Japanese (under the guidance of scarcely a hundred American operatives), and it dropped several hundred turned Axis POWs back into Germany to gather intelligence at the end of the war.

Donovan was willing to lead from the front: During the Normandy landings, Donovan and an aide made their way onto Utah Beach, where they were promptly pinned down by machine-gun fire. Both of them knew about Allied penetration of Axis codes, one of the most closely guarded secrets of the war. Donovan unholstered his pistol and told his aide that he would shoot him first, then himself. "After all, I am the commanding officer," he said. But they made it back to the ship safely.

One of the OSS's biggest coups was Operation Sunrise, a successful secret attempt to broker an early end to the Italian campaign without arousing Stalin's suspicions. It arguably saved thousands of Allied lives. But there was more to it than that. By arranging a separate peace with the German troops in northern Italy, and by illegally engineering the escape of thousands of Gestapo and SS officers, the OSS laid the groundwork for the CIA's spying during the Cold War. It certainly recruited some objectionable resources, but as John Foster Dulles once said, "For us there are two sorts of people in the world: there are those who are Christians and support free enterprise and there are the others."

Other interesting ramifications came with OSS activities in

Southeast Asia. Extensive preparations were made for an uprising in Thailand, with two OSS majors camped out in an empty palace in Bangkok, shuttling back and forth in curtained limousines under the noses of Japanese guards. Thailand had actually declared war on the Allies after Pearl Harbor, but the OSS was training the sizable "Free Thai" underground movement for an uprising. The war ended before action could be taken.

In Vietnam, on the other hand, the OSS briefly supported Ho Chi Minh's battle against the Japanese. In September 1945, the Vietnamese declaration of independence opened with the words: "All men are created equal. They are endowed by their Creator with certain inalienable rights, among these are Life, Liberty, and the pursuit of Happiness."

It is tempting to wonder what the postwar American intelligence agency might have been like had Donovan and his OSS not been ousted unceremoniously and eventually replaced with the CIA. As one historical account published internally by the CIA described it:

"Due to an oversight in the drafting of Executive Order 9621, Donovan had just ten days to dismantle his sprawling agency. He was too busy to do much about saving the components of OSS bound for the War Department. Donovan microfilmed his office files and bade farewell to his troops at a September 28, 1945, rally in a converted skating rink down the hill from his headquarters at 2430 E Street, NW:

"'We have come to the end of an unusual experiment. This experiment was to determine whether a group of Americans constituting a cross section of racial origins, of abilities, temperaments and talents could meet and risk an encounter with the long-established and well-trained enemy organizations…. You can go with the assurance that you have made a beginning in showing the people of America that only by decisions of national policy based upon accurate information can we have the chance of a peace that will endure.'"

ALLEN DULLES

CIA SPYMASTER

▶

Allen Dulles led a distinguished career as a CIA spymaster, a career that was, however, bookended by two intelligence debacles.

In April 1917, while on duty in one of his first diplomatic postings in Bern, Switzerland, he chose to brush off a request for a meeting with a man named Vladimir I. Lenin in favor of a lunchtime tennis date. The next day, the Germans allowed Lenin to cross their territory and return to Russia. The dangerous revolutionary traveled in a boxcar, "like a plague bacillus," as Churchill later described it.

The incident that ended his career was the 1961 Bay of Pigs, a notoriously unsuccessful attempt to overthrow Fidel Castro; JFK fired Dulles a few months after it backfired.

He has been called, variously, "undoubtedly the greatest U.S. professional intelligence officer of his time" and "the most dangerous man in the world."

Although he never fulfilled his ambition to become the Dulles family's third secretary of state (that honor fell to his older brother, John Foster) his career was certainly filled with coups, literally. Two of the best known were the American-aided overthrow of Iran's leader Mohammad Mosaddeq, after he attempted to nationalize the nation's huge oil industry (1953), and the ouster of Guatemala's president, Jacobo Arbenz (1954), who was believed to threaten the huge American conglomerate United Fruit.

He also oversaw the development of the ultra-high-flying U2 spy plane, which provided a considerable flow of intelligence but also led to a diplomatic embarrassment when the Soviet Union shot one down in 1960. After retiring, Dulles served on the Warren Commission, investigating the assassination of President Kennedy.

Dulles was ultimately fired over the Bay of Pigs plan to overthrow Castro.

"Sex and espionage certainly go together—that's an old tradition." Markus W

MARKUS WOLF

EAST GERMAN SPYMASTER

John le Carré rather pointedly told one interviewer that Markus Wolf had not been the model for his larger-than-life and twice-as-sinister spymaster, Karla. It is not surprising that the question was asked: The East German spymaster Markus Johannes Wolf (nicknamed Mischa, a nod to his lifelong connections with Moscow) at one point ran as many as 3,000 agents in West Germany during the Cold War.

One of his most successful operations was the "secretaries offensive," in which he unleashed a succession of "Red Casanovas" to prey on lonely spinsters working in West German government offices. He had, of course, a historically rich array of targets—eligible German men were in short supply after the war. Wolf refined the historic Russian use of "Romeo spies"—primarily used as tools of blackmail—and focused on the longer-lasting benefits of making the targets fall in love. The KGB followed in Wolf's footsteps, and the cynicism of the technique became evident when Leonore Heinz, secretary to a department head in the Bonn foreign ministry, began to spy at the request of her new husband. When their KGB contact defected, Leonore Heinz was arrested and shown proof that her husband had married her at his superior's orders. She later hanged herself in her cell.

Wolf's single most spectacular penetration agent, however, was Günther Guillaume. The son of a doctor who had treated future West German Chancellor Willy Brandt, Guillaume staged an escape from East Germany in 1956, spying until he was arrested in 1974. In that quarter century, he became Brandt's closest aide; his arrest was sufficiently embarrassing that Brandt was forced to resign. Guillaume's reports were regularly read by Soviet Foreign Minister Andrei Gromyko, and gave the Russians important insight into West German foreign policy.

THEY DID IT FOR THE MONEY

L ike the happy families described in Tolstoy's *Anna Karenina,* idealistic spies could be said to be all alike, while every mercenary spy is mercenary in his or her own way.

John Walker was arguably mercenary for the sake of being mercenary; Alfred Redl left a suicide note attributing his treason to "levity and passion." Benedict Arnold was very happy to take the equivalent in today's money of about a million dollars in cash, but he also seethed with resentment at the failure of his superiors to give him the promotions he felt were due him, or to bestow them quickly enough. Some of the spies were tangled in various toils: The Snowman described in the book and movie *The Falcon and the Snowman* was a cocaine addict, hence his nickname. Robert Hanssen, protagonist of one of the most spectacular cases of treachery in FBI history, had been thwarted repeatedly as a child and seemed to revel in an almost infantile acting-out, but one with tragically adult consequences, as one American spy in Russia after another was caught and executed, thanks to Hanssen's well-compensated tips.

BENEDICT ARNOLD

BRITISH SPY AND TRAITOR

Every career brings frustrations, but Benedict Arnold reacted—it is generally agreed—badly. Admittedly, Arnold started out with a pretty strong sense of entitlement: He was actually Benedict Arnold IV, bearing the name of a great-grandfather who served three terms as colonial governor of Rhode Island. And at first he seemed content to be a merchant, running a combination drugstore and bookshop and trading with the West Indies. But once the Revolutionary War got under way, Arnold's military and political ambitions were kindled.

He was clearly very brave and energetic. He was severely wounded in a 1775 assault on Quebec. He commanded a flotilla on Lake Champlain that took on a superior British fleet in the first naval engagement of the war, fought the fleet to a standstill with one surviving ship, ran aground, and escaped on foot. He was a victor in the crucial Battle of Saratoga, and the commander of occupied Philadelphia.

But each of these triumphs and victories seemed to bring with it a lawsuit, a censure, or a board of inquiry. While he was generally acquitted, each of these investigations involved months and months of delay. The last one resulted in a reprimand—albeit in the friendliest, most approving terms—from General Washington.

And it was then that Arnold, one of the most admired soldiers of the Revolution, became a British spy. The greatest treasure that he brought to his handlers were the plans of West Point, where he was now commander. The agreed payment was nearly a million dollars in modern money. But the deal went awry: Arnold's handler, Maj. John André, was arrested with the plans to the strategic fort in his boots, tried, and hanged. Arnold escaped and died in exile.

Arnold was a war hero and patriot who became a traitor for the money.

Redl was handed a pistol by fellow officers upon being discovered as a sp

ALFRED REDL

BLACKMAILED into the GAME

In *The Panther's Feast*, military historian Robert Asprey describes the meeting at which then-Capt. Alfred Redl, a highly placed intelligence officer in the Austro-Hungarian military service, became a double agent.

Dressed in civilian clothes and wearing a heavy overcoat with a fur collar, Redl made his way cautiously up a steep, winding dirt path into the Vienna hills, a heavy walking stick in hand. Breathing heavily and by this point badly frightened, he realized that he had been lured far from inconvenient witnesses to a spot where he had clearly not been followed. In Asprey's reconstruction, Redl there encounters a man in a black overcoat with a turned-up collar and a hat pulled low over his face. With a pistol in one hand and an envelope containing ten thousand crowns in banknotes in the other, the man offered Redl a choice: either become a Russian spy, or have his secret exposed. Against a backdrop of leafless trees, with the gentle whine of wind in his ears, Redl pondered. "Don't you understand the dirty trick that society has played on you, Redl?" the man cajoled. "Do you think I care if you are a homosexual?... Society has trapped you, Alfred Redl. I am offering you escape."

Although this is a fictional account, former CIA chief Allen Dulles praised the book highly, saying that it "stays very close to the historical facts." Whatever the exact details of Redl's recruitment, he did become a Russian spy, "Russia's most productive spy in the Austro-Hungarian military establishment," as one respected historian of espionage called him. It is generally accepted that Redl was a homosexual who was blackmailed into cooperating, and it is generally thought that in the years between his shadowy meeting in the hills and his despairing suicide, caught as a spy and handed a loaded pistol by his fellow officers, the Russian spies that he caught were fed to him by his spymaster, Nikolai Batyushin. In exchange, Redl gave the Russians a great deal of information, most famously and most damagingly, Austrian codes and general staff mobilization plans. It is thought that the Austrian attack on Serbia in August 1914 failed in part because the Russians passed the Austrian plans to the Serbs, a Slavic ally. He also enhanced his reputation as an effective counterintelligence officer by falsifying evidence against fellow officers.

Although there is little doubt that Redl was a Russian agent, there is reason to believe that another, ghostly figure may have been feeding the Russians information as well: "No. 25" was the Russians' code name for a prominent figure inside the Austrian general staff. But "No. 25" was recruited by a different Russian officer, and the only Russian officer who knew him personally later insisted that "No. 25" was not Redl. It has even been suggested that Redl, as a homosexual, may have been set up by the Austrian intelligence services. In any case, "No. 25" disappeared soon thereafter.

In the years before he was turned, Redl had been a formidable and innovative intelligence officer. He used hidden cameras as spy tools, and gramophones surreptitiously to record interrogations; he used fingerprints to break a Russian spy ring.

Ironically, Redl was caught through a mail-monitoring system that he himself had put in place. He was arrested after picking up two letters containing cash—and nothing else—from a post office box in Vienna. And it had been his replacement, Maximilian Ronge, working with systems that Redl had perfected, who captured him. His paymasters had used return addresses known to correspond to French and Russian intelligence operatives in the countries where the

Redl's homosexuality became the leverage that the Russians used to turn him into a mole.

envelopes had been mailed. Confronted by his fellow officers, given a pistol, and left alone in a room, he wrote two letters, one to his brother and one to his superior officer. Among his last words: "Levity and passion have destroyed me. Pray for me. I pay with my life for my sins." He then shot himself.

SIDNEY REILLY

GREATEST SPY IN HISTORY

Reilly was either the greatest spy in history or a liar.

Sidney Reilly—the "Ace of Spies"—is considered by some to have been the greatest spy in history. By others, he is considered to have been a pathological liar. He was unquestionably courageous, deceitful, inventive, and dangerous to everyone he knew, especially himself.

It begins with the name: Sigmund Rosenblum, the son of a Jewish physician from Vienna and a Russian woman who was otherwise engaged, in fact otherwise married, to a Russian colonel who frequented the imperial court.

Psychologists could have a field day with his early years—he abandoned Russia after learning of his illegitimate birth, and then rescued the lives of (variously, in his accounts) two or three British officers, who rewarded him with a British passport.

He moved to England and made the first of his three bigamous marriages: the other two were to a Russian woman named Nadine Massino and an actress named Pepita Bobadilla.

In a life that seemed like a cross between Reds and Zelig, Reilly hopscotched across Eurasia for almost 30 years until his execution in 1925, operating as a British agent under the code name ST1. Some claim that Ian Fleming based his character James Bond on Reilly.

His career is thought to have begun in the East End of London, spying on anti-czarist refugees; from there he went on to spy on the Germans or the Dutch during the Boer War. He may have worked under cover as a welder in the Krupp weapons works in Germany.

He appeared in Port Arthur next, on Russia's Pacific coast, and may have been linked with the devastating Japanese surprise attack that humbled the Russian navy. He then helped the British to secure oil interests in Persia and made a small fortune as an intermediary for German shipbuilders, while stealing the ship plans for Britain.

His exploits before and during the Bolshevik revolution and in the civil war that followed were legendary, but his reports became increasingly unreliable. He was finally trapped by a false-front anti-Soviet subversive group known as the Trust, while in Russia under cover, and executed.

ELYESA BAZNA

CODE NAME "CICERO"

To say that no man is a hero to his own valet hardly begins to cover the details of the Cicero case. Cicero was the German code name for Elyesa Bazna, a valet in the Ankara residence of British Ambassador Sir Hughe Knatchbull-Hugessen, who had been nicknamed, in his turn, "Snatch" by his well-born schoolmates at Eton and Balliol. The German ambassador to neutral Turkey, Franz von Papen, is said to have chosen the code name Cicero in recognition of Bazna's "astonishing eloquence"; "Snatch," on the other hand, may simply have been based on the first syllable of the ambassador's surname.

If there was a battle of wits between the two, Snatch did not seem to have been aware of the fact. He was lulled into trusting Bazna, according to a new set of documents released in early 2005, by Bazna's fine singing voice. He further discounted Bazna as a danger because he was "too stupid" and spoke no English. Bazna may indeed have spoken no English—though that is a risky assumption on which to base security decisions—but he was smart enough to have trained as a locksmith. And the German ambassador in Ankara dubbed Bazna Cicero because of his "astonishing eloquence."

How smooth was he? Well, historian Joseph Persico describes him as a "swarthy, compact Albanian in his forties, heavily browed and black-moustachioed," but in the movie made from his postwar auto-biography, I Was Cicero, he is played by the exquisitely creepy James Mason. Swarthy, but slick, in other words.

As a locksmith, he was able to make wax impressions of the keys to the various colored boxes—brown and red, in the ambassadorial residence—that contained sensitive documents. While Snatch took

Cicero gave information to the Germans
about the Normandy invasion, but they refused to believe it.

his morning bath (no doubt warbling like Bertie Wooster as he splashed in the tub), Bazna would unlock the document box and photograph everything that looked useful. In the afternoon he had a second chance, while the ambassador tickled the ivories in the next room. As soon as the piano-playing stopped, Bazna would replace the papers and relock the box.

Among the materials that Bazna secured for the Germans was the code name Overlord—but apparently nothing more—for the impending Normandy invasion. There were various planning documents from Moscow, Cairo, and Tehran, as well as Snatch's Christmas list and private correspondence with King George VI, and even a telegram from the Foreign Office warning that the embassy had a security problem.

A recent British government analysis of the Cicero case noted that there were four potential areas of damage from Bazna's work in late 1943 and early 1944: tipping the Germans off to planning for Overlord; helping them to influence the Turkish decision against allowing the British to establish airfields on Turkish soil to tip the balance in the Dodecanese; helping Nazi code-breakers to penetrate a British cipher; and reassuring the Germans that the Allies had no intention of moving into the Balkans.

On Turkish diplomacy and the British cipher, no harm seems to have been done. On Overlord, fortunately, the higher-echelon Nazis proved that they could be every bit as obtuse as their high-born enemies. The British report noted that once the Germans came to the conclusion that Cicero's documents were not merely misinformation, Nazi Foreign Minister Ribbentrop "thought the documents showed fault lines in the Allied coalition, an interpretation that countered SS chief Heinrich Himmler's right-hand-man Walter Schellenberg's rather more reasoned viewpoint that the documents pointed, however vaguely, to a massive Allied invasion of Europe and the destruction of Germany." Oops.

On the last point, the British government study says that an entry from Wehrmacht chief of operations Gen. Alfred Jodl's diary and a statement from Ambassador von Papen suggest that Bazna's work reassured them that no Balkans invasion was in the works. If so, it concludes, "perhaps Cicero earned all the money that the Germans paid him." A more ironic spin may be detected if we reflect that in point of fact, the Germans paid Cicero in counterfeit currency—a fine twist of the knife in the back of a hardworking spy. That betrayal took a long time to emerge: Bazna was not arrested for possession of counterfeit currency until after the war.

And what about Snatch, or Sir Hughe, as he is more respectfully termed? He was shuttled off to be ambassador to newly liberated Brussels until 1947, and then seems to have spent the rest of his life defending his reputation.

The latest documents, released 35 years after the deaths—within a year of each other—of Sir Hughe and Elyesa Bazna, won't be helping Sir Hughe's standing in posterity. At the time the leaks were discovered, apparently, Sir Hughe first blamed the Turkish government, but was then obliged to confess that he left a case with the briefing papers for the Cairo conference unattended on the train while he visited the restaurant car. A Foreign Office official commented wearily: "We must recognize that His Excellency does not habitually differentiate between convenience and security."

In one particularly wry commentary on the deaths of Sir Hughe and his overinquisitive valet, one writer observed, "Cicero was never caught, and died in 1970—within a year of Sir Hughe—in Munich, where he worked as a night watchman. But at least no one ever forced him to go to Belgium."

CHRISTOPHER BOYCE

THE FALCON, MINUS THE SNOWMAN

His partner's poor impulse control infuriated Boyce's Russian handlers and contributed to the Falcon's ultimate capture.

The extended career of Christopher Boyce, who sold the Soviets information about American spy-satellite technology that ultimately derailed the SALT arms-control treaties, says a great deal about what was wrong with the seventies.

Aside from the hobbies (Boyce was into falconry, and Andrew Lee, his partner in the spying, was an avid pot and coke hound; they were dubbed the Falcon and the Snowman in the best-selling book and the movie that chronicled the pair's misdeeds), there are the drinks.

Boyce, despite being a college dropout, managed to secure a relatively low-paying job at the government contractor TRW. In a classic misstep, TRW gave an underpaid, underqualified employee access to some of its most closely guarded secrets. Boyce regularly spent time in the "black vault," where TRW regularly uploaded satellite information from its California facilities to the CIA. There, Boyce and his colleagues regularly used a cipher-destroying machine to mix banana daiquiris. Not in itself illegal, but certainly objectionable.

Much more serious, Boyce had used his pal, Lee, as a courier in a plot to sell secrets to the U.S.S.R., with meetings in Mexico City. Together, the two passed secrets in exchange for some 70,000 dollars. They were caught as a result of Lee's poor impulse control (his erratic behavior so infuriated their KGB handler that he once threw Lee from a moving car; apparently the lesson didn't stick). The Mexican police noticed Lee (played in the movie by an unusually truculent Sean Penn) toss a note over the gate of the Soviet compound. When they arrested him, they found strips of film of top-secret documents.

There was almost a fairy-tale ending to Boyce's story. He managed to escape from the prison facility at Lompoc, California, by cutting through the ten-foot-high chain-link fence. He lived by robbing banks, purchased a 29-foot sailboat, and was learning to fly in a bid to reach Russia when he was recaptured.

JOHN WALKER

A FAMILY AFFAIR

The comedy group Monty Python used to stage a competition for the "Worst Family in Britain." The family of John A. Walker, Jr., might have considered giving up their U.S. citizenship to compete. But then again, there was no money in the prize.

The dysfunctionality of the Walker family boggles the imagination. John Walker (who loved to order the scotch that shared his name) recruited his brother and his son as key members of his spy ring. He tried to recruit his daughter into the ring, encouraging her to have an abortion, as a baby would only interfere with her espionage activities. Walker's wife, Barbara, had an affair with his brother, Arthur, in the years that John was beginning his career as a spy. John Walker had joined the Navy after dropping out of high school, only to avoid prosecution for a string of serious burglaries. As his debts mounted, he tried to persuade his wife to become a prostitute to increase his cash flow. And to cap the dysfunctionality, it was Barbara who tipped off the FBI: She had previously made two drunken phone calls to the bureau, but had been ignored. In 1984 she succeeded, and the following year, the entire ring was arrested.

The only decent family interaction, perhaps, was John's willingness to plea bargain in order to obtain a reduced sentence for his son, Michael (now free). That deal came at a high cost to one non-Walker member of the ring, Jerry Whitworth. He was sentenced to 365 years in prison and fined almost a half million dollars. He will be eligible for parole at age 107.

As dispiriting as the story of Walker's 18-year career as a spy was, it was a stunning success for his Russian handlers. The KGB station chief in Washington shouted out, "I want this!" as he read

John Walker tried to recruit his entire family into his spy ring.

Walker's first sample of material. Walker was considered the most important U.S. spy until Aldrich Ames, and was made an admiral in the Soviet navy. And the electronic codes and diagrams he furnished the Soviets doubled the value of materials that fell into their hands after the fall of South Vietnam and the capture of the spy ship the U.S.S. *Pueblo*.

RON PELTON

SINKING IVY BELLS ➤

If you visit the KGB museum in the Lubyanka building—former KGB headquarters, a site with a grim reputation—one item on exhibit is a large cylindrical "pod," part of an operation code-named Ivy Bells. In Ivy Bells, U.S. Navy submarines would enter the Sea of Okhotsk, off the peninsula of Kamchatka, at the extreme eastern tip of the former Soviet Union, and lower electronic canisters, or pods, weighing several tons, to the seabed. There divers would fasten alligator clips to an underwater Soviet cable, and the pod would record several weeks of transmissions. The Soviets were so confident that the cable was invulnerable to Western intercepts that they often sent messages in a less secure code, and sometimes in plain, uncoded versions.

Ivy Bells was the brainchild of a naval intelligence officer, who grew up near the Mississippi River. He reasoned that the Russians would post "underwater cable" warning signs just like those he had seen in his childhood. Sure enough, those Soviet cable warning signs pointed the way to the most improbable wiretap operation imaginable.

One day in 1981, overhead surveillance showed a cluster of Soviet ships directly over the pod site; when the submarine returned to pick up the pod, it was gone (only to reappear in the KGB museum).

The mystery of how Ivy Bells' cover was blown was not solved until 1985, with the defection (and subsequent re-defection) of Vitaly Yurchenko, who helped to identify Ronald Pelton, a 14-year NSA (National Security Agency) intelligence analyst who had an inconvenient personal bankruptcy to resolve and a handy gift: a photographic memory. Pelton contacted the Russians (it was a wiretap tape of his phone call that allowed a colleague to identify his voice) and became a walk-in spy. He betrayed four other major NSA programs besides Ivy Bells.

...elton received $40,000 from the Soviets and three life sentences from the Feds.

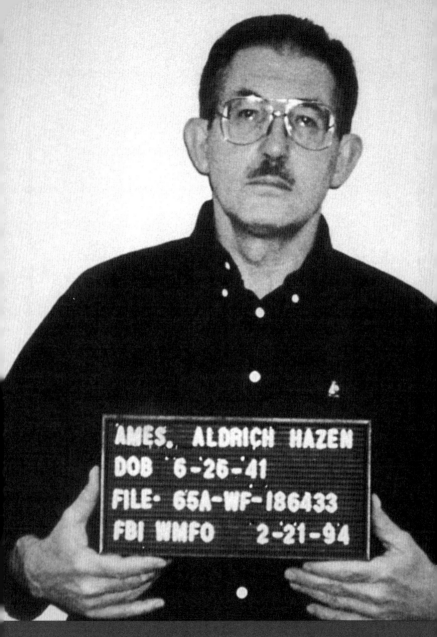

At least ten CIA assets inside the Soviet Union were executed because of Ame

ALDRICH AMES

LIVING THE HIGH LIFE

One writer, referring to the encounter between Aldrich Ames and Vitaly Yurchenko as an "amorality tale" and a venture into a "gravity-free zone," pointed out that one Soviet official said that the whole episode made him feel physically ill.

But then, the writer (Brian Cathcart) went on to say, even the Soviet official's claim to a queasy stomach might have been for show. Or, Cathcart ventures, maybe the official was "just dizzy, like the rest of us."

Yurchenko's story is told in detail elsewhere in this volume, but Cathcart makes an observation that certainly extends to the life of Aldrich Ames, a CIA counterintelligence officer responsible for the most damaging penetration in the agency's history. As a result of Ames's spying, at least ten CIA assets—all Russians or Eastern Europeans—inside the Soviet Union were executed; he blew more than a hundred covert operations, revealed the names of at least 30 Western spies, and identified many of the U.S. agents operating in the Soviet Union (or, toward the end of his career, Russia).

The details that made the Soviet official's gorge rise were these: Yurchenko defected, and when he was being debriefed, one of the debriefers was Ames, a Soviet spy. Yurchenko then re-defected back to the Soviet Union. Gravity-free zone, indeed.

When Ames began spying in April 1985, a walk-in to the Soviet Embassy, he had only intended to get money by betraying three American assets in the U.S.S.R. whom he knew to be double agents. Or at least that is what he later claimed: The Soviets would have been obliged to pay him the 50,000 dollars he was demanding or else admit that the supposed U.S. agents were actually working for them.

But according to one retired KGB officer, there were two double agents working for the U.S. in the package of goods Ames first unloaded; they were both later executed.

One of the CIA counterintelligence officers who was crucial in identifying Ames as a Soviet mole was Sandy Grimes. She paints a pretty vivid picture of how the suspicions hardened.

She recalled that she and Rick, as she called Ames, had come up in the agency around the same time, in the early seventies: "We were young case officers together, we grew up together, we car-pooled. I had seen what I always called the old Rick.... He was a nice guy." But the transition, she said, began during Ames's tour in Rome. "When he came back from Rome he was just a different person.... It wasn't the capped teeth, it wasn't the clean fingernails, it wasn't the Italian suits and the six hundred dollar shoes and the silk men's hose. His posture was different. Rick always had been a slob and slouched and couldn't care less what he looked like, but he stood erect, he sat erect, there was an arrogance that was just...he exuded arrogance."

Sandy Grimes also recalled some of the discussion among CIA employees. One of her fellow operatives, Diana Worthen, had served with Ames and his second wife, Rosario, whom Ames met in Mexico City. Worthen knew that Rosario had no money. Sandy Grimes went on, "So when Rick and Rosario come back to the United States from their tour in Rome and Rick is telling everybody this is Rosario's money, well Diana was saying that no, Rosario didn't have any money, where was it coming from?" They speculated that, since Rosario's father had died, perhaps they had received an inheritance or a settlement. But there was a telltale detail, according to Grimes: "Rosario's mother still worked, and in my experience, wealthy Latin women don't work."

It would have been impossible to miss the sudden appearance of money in Ames's everyday life. He and his wife earned almost three million dollars in their spying careers. Despite an evident drinking problem and a salary of less than 70,000 dollars, he was spending with ostentatious recklessness. He bought a $40,000 Jaguar XJ6, and as if to underline the point, the car was red. He bought a $540,000 home—when that kind of money bought a lot of house in Washington, D.C.—and in what ought to have been a dead giveaway, if anyone had been paying attention, he paid for it in cash.

As William F. Buckley wrote a few years later, "Ames disguised himself about as subtly as King Kong, but it seemed that there was nothing he could do blatant enough to attract the attention of the agency." Ames was scornful of his fellow spy catchers, but Buckley adds a poignant detail about the one eventuality Ames did fear: "that friends of the men he was betraying, month after month, would notice the gory disappearance of a member of the resistance and advise Washington."

And some voices were raised even there, but as Aldrich Ames himself described it, "The CIA has become a vast institutionalized machine that cranks material out endlessly and is very easy for senior policy-makers to ignore."

Given that kind of bureaucratic sense of futility, perhaps we have a context in which to understand why Ames should have done what he did. He himself doesn't seem to know: "I mean, you might as well ask why a middle-aged man with no criminal record might go and put a paper bag over his head and rob a bank…. It's kind of dramatic, and perhaps interesting, but when you get right down to it, kind of a banal answer."

Aldrich Ames worked for the Soviets as a mole for nine years and is now serving a life sentence without parole.

Pitts resorted to selling secrets for cash because New York was so expensi

EARL EDWIN PITTS

COST-OF-LIVING INCREASE

The *New York Times* reported on the Earl Pitts spy case in 1997 with glee: "New York made him do it." Pitts, a former FBI counterintelligence agent, was sentenced to 27 years in jail for feeding secrets to the Soviet Union in exchange for a quarter million dollars. When asked in an interview from jail what he would have done differently, if he could only change the past, Pitts replied, "I wouldn't have gone to New York."

If it's not the cost of living in the Pitts story, it's the constant battle for a green card. Pitts's initial Soviet contact at the UN, Rollan Dzheikiya, later retired from government service and contacted the FBI in hopes of obtaining a green card for himself. It is not recorded whether he received it, but his part of the deal was handing over Pitts to his American handlers.

Ironically, the year after Pitts moved to New York, the FBI instituted a cost-of-living increase for agents in high-price areas, as well as moving compensation. But it was too late; he had already begun selling secrets to the Russians, betraying his country for cash.

It was easy for Pitts to meet with his handlers, because his job was to recruit Russians as spies for the U.S. Still, his tradecraft wasn't particularly good. One crucial piece of evidence against him was a computer disk from his portable computer, recommending dead drops for the coming year. Apparently Pitts believed that it would be impossible for investigators to retrieve information from a laptop.

Years after he had gone dormant, FBI agents deceived Pitts into thinking that they were Russians, reactivating him. He passed secrets to them and accepted almost 65,000 dollars in exchange. Each transaction was captured on film.

ROBERT HANSSEN

TURNCOAT AND TRAITOR

When Robert Hanssen—later to become a FBI agent and, in time, a Soviet spy—was just a boy, his father abused him physically, wrapping him tightly in a blanket and spinning him around so forcefully that the centrifugal force made little Robert vomit. Howard Hanssen, a Chicago cop, continued to abuse him over the years. On the day that a teenage Robert Hanssen took the test for his driver's license, his father surreptitiously bribed the examiner to flunk him.

When Howard Hanssen met Bonnie Wauck, his son's fiancée, he reportedly asked her, "Why are you marrying this guy?"

Just a few days after their wedding, she got a nasty surprise: An old girlfriend called up to inform her that she and Hanssen had just made love.

The victim was beginning to victimize.

You could argue endlessly about the reasons a person like Hanssen becomes a turncoat and a traitor. Whatever the significance of these factors, however, it would be almost impossible to deny that Robert Hanssen had a difficult, twisted childhood, and that he became a difficult, twisted adult.

The past has many different ways of influencing the present, and another remarkably painful legacy was running on a parallel track to Hanssen's.

Tom Kimmel was one of the FBI's top counterintelligence experts and was nearing retirement in late 1998. Buffs of intelligence history will recognize Kimmel's surname. His grandfather, the improbably named Husband Kimmel, was the admiral in charge of the U.S. Pacific Fleet in December 1941. He was relieved of his

anssen was arrested after planting a bag full of intelligence at a dead drop.

command within days, his career ruined, and subjected to a congressional investigation. At the end of 1998, Tom Kimmel wrote a report, which he presented in a briefing in January 1999 to FBI chief Louis Freeh, stating his belief that there was a mole within the FBI. The report did not meet with the director's favor; Freeh was preparing to retire, and the last thing he would have wanted to add to a list of problems that included the Waco–Branch Davidian massacre, the Oklahoma City bombing case, and the Atlanta Olympics bombing snafu was a Russian mole within the agency. Kimmel's report was denigrated and largely ignored.

Time passed. In the late fall of 2000, Congress passed a bill recommending that Husband Kimmel be restored posthumously to his rank and absolved of all blame. And in February 2001—even before Freeh could safely retire—Robert Hanssen was arrested just after he placed a garbage bag full of valuable intelligence at a dead drop in a Virginia park.

They were bittersweet vindications for Kimmel. A cloud continues to lower over his grandfather's reputation (President Bill Clinton rejected the congressional recommendation to reinstate Kimmel's rank), and the damage that Hanssen did, the deaths he caused, cannot be undone.

Investigators called Robert Hanssen "the most damaging spy in FBI history." The Russians paid him over $ 600,000 in cash and diamonds to spy. But the path to that catastrophic betrayal was a twisting one. One reviewer called Hanssen "a spy for all reasons."

One reason may have been frustration. When Hanssen finally made it to what he saw as the big time—counterespionage against the Soviets in New York City—he figured out that the Soviets did most of their spying activity on the weekends, when the FBI was off-duty. He organized a major sweep to catch the Russian agents in the act, but, as one of Hanssen's friends later recalled, "Well over half of the FBI guys called in from home. They didn't want to work on Sunday. The Russians got away."

Another motive may have lain in Hanssen's never-sated need for an audience and approval, which dime-store psychology might trace back to his father's relentless disapproval. The Russians were immensely appreciative of Hanssen's work, and paid him extra. He received a letter of commendation from the chief of the KGB, along with confirmation of a deposit of $100,000 in a Russian bank. It was a pretty simple equation, at least to someone operating in an alternate moral universe. When Hanssen resumed contact with the Russians after an extended hiatus, they knew the kind of response he wanted: "Dear friend: welcome! We express our sincere joy on the occasion of resumption of contact with you."

Whether that joy was sincere or not, the Russians had every reason to consider Hanssen a friend. Not only did he hand over information betraying entire systems of espionage, but the incompetence of FBI and CIA investigations managed to neutralize another veteran CIA officer, whose career was basically ruined while he was under scrutiny, with the code name Gray Deceiver, as the suspected mole. Adding further damage, a book on Hanssen openly named the man code-named Gray Deceiver, despite the fact that he was still working as a CIA operative, and despite a letter from CIA Director George Tenet to the chairman of Random House asking that the name be kept secret.

A further layer of weirdness to the Hanssen story comes with the sex angle. Hanssen had a number of kinks, one of which was to spend money on a stripper—giving her jewels, an expensive car, and a credit card—but never sleeping with her. He also regularly showed videotapes of himself having sex with his wife to a friend.

PATRIOTS AND TRAITORS

pies who work because of their beliefs, or "altruistic" spies, run the gamut from genuine, if somewhat inept, patriots (Nathan Hale, who was hanged during his first mission) to spies like Kim Philby, who betrayed their family, their colleagues, and their country, but did so because of strongly held beliefs. Two of the spies discussed here were actually working to put nuclear weapons in the hands of Joseph Stalin, an arguably psychopathic dictator. It is interesting, in exploring the gray world of espionage, to compare the Rosenbergs with Richard Sorge, another of Stalin's outstanding agents. Sorge enabled Stalin to focus on defeating--indeed, pulverizing--the German Sixth Army at the siege of Stalingrad, by providing intelligence that the Japanese did not intend to attack from the east. A further interesting portrait of idealism in espionage can be seen in the story of Pham Xuan An, a respected correspondent for various American news publications, but also a leading spy and strategist for the North Vietnamese Army.

NATHAN HALE

ONE LIFE TO LOSE

As Hale stood with a noose around his neck, he spoke the words with which he has gone down in history: "I only regret that I have but one life to lose for my country."

Nathan Hale was the first American to be executed for spying for his country, and a statue of him stands outside the CIA's original headquarters. In an inadvertent irony, Hale represents bravery and selfless sacrifice, but also—as recently unearthed documents reveal—monumentally poor tradecraft.

Following a disastrous American defeat at the Battle of Long Island, General Washington asked for volunteers to go behind British lines to spy. Lt. James Sprague, a veteran of the French and Indian Wars, made a revealing statement, expressing the views of his fellow officers: "I am willing to go and fight them. But as far as going among them and being taken and hung up like a dog, I will not do it."

But Hale expressed his views to a friend: "I wish to be useful, and every kind of service, necessary to the public good, becomes honorable by being necessary. If the exigencies of my country demand a peculiar service, its claims to perform that service become imperious." And so he stepped forward, the sole volunteer.

Hale was a tall young man with noticeable scars on his face from a gunpowder blast. He had been a schoolteacher before the revolution, and so he chose a natural enough cover: He claimed to be a Tory (or British sympaththizer) schoolteacher in search of a job, and carried his Yale diploma as proof of his qualifications. He wore a suit of "brown Holland cloth" and a round, broad-brimmed hat. He removed the silver buckles from his shoes, noting that "they would not comport with his supposed calling."

So far, so good, except for the obvious problem with using genuine identification papers bearing one's real name. Indeed, until 2003, nothing certain was known about Nathan Hale's capture, but one of the most likely theories was that Hale's cousin, Samuel Hale, a New Hampshire Tory and commissary of prisoners, had been summoned because of the similarity of names, and had identified him as a revolutionary.

But documents recently donated to the Library of Congress tell a different story. An account written during or shortly after the Revolutionary War by Consider Tiffany, an improbably named Tory shopkeeper, states that Maj. Robert Rogers, a cunning British officer, had been observing Hale for a couple of days. Rogers changed into civilian dress and engaged Hale in conversation, persuading him that Rogers himself was "upon the business of spying out the inclination of the people and motion of the British troops." He thus persuaded Hale to admit that he, too, was a spy. As Hale relaxed with his new co-conspirators—now witnesses to his confession—they arrested him. General Howe ordered Hale hanged without benefit of trial.

RICHARD SORGE

AKA STALIN'S SPY

It was as if Richard Sorge was fated to be a spy. He was born into ideological royalty, as it were. His great-uncle had been a secretary to Karl Marx. His father was German, his mother, Russian, and so he could pass as either. He was seriously injured and awarded the Iron Cross for his service to Germany in World War I; but in the next war he would play a far different role.

While convalescing, he studied Marxism and became a Communist. Before long, he left for Moscow and became a young agent of the Comintern. He spent a few years collecting intelligence in Germany, and then returned to Russia, where, after moving up through the ranks of the nascent KGB, he was sent to Shanghai.

It was there that he met notorious, Missouri-born triple agent Agnes Smedley. The pair became lovers and colleagues. Smedley introduced him to Ozaki Hotsumi, a Japanese newspaperman and Communist who ultimately infiltrated the Japanese cabinet.

In 1933 Sorge was sent to Japan to form an espionage ring; he stopped off in Germany first to establish his bona fides as a newspaper reporter. Once he reached Japan, he successfully insinuated himself into the German Embassy and the Japanese government.

His greatest achievements were to give the Soviet Union advance warning of Operation Barbarossa (the German invasion of Russia) and to pass intelligence that suggested an impending Japanese attack on the U.S., just before Pearl Harbor. There was a crucial link between the two invaluable pieces of information—the Japanese focus on war against the United States provided assurance that they would not be attacking the Soviet Union, thus helping their German allies with a second front.

Stalin had been dead for years when Richard Sorge, often described as "Stalin's Spy," was posthumously named a Hero of the Soviet Union.

Though Stalin seems to have ignored the warning on Barbarossa (the Soviet dictator wanted to postpone war and feared a provocation; he gave orders not to react, so German troops pouring over the border encountered little or no resistance in the first 12 hours), the assurance that Japan would not attack from the east let the Russians concentrate their armies, successfully defending Moscow. Sorge was arrested in November 1941, before his warnings on the Pearl Harbor attack proved accurate. He and his fellow spy, Ozaki Hotsumi, were held for nearly three years in a Japanese prison. After repeated Soviet refusals to exchange the master spy for Japanese POWs, Sorge was hanged in November 1944.

Garcia believed that helping the Allies would hasten Franco's demise.

JUAN PUJOL GARCIA

BEST DOUBLE AGENT, CLASS of '45

On D-Day plus 4 (June 10, 1944) a jubilant Winston Churchill walked into the London control room for the invasion operation. It had just been reported that Hitler had canceled the transfer of German troops to Normandy. As one witness recalled the scene, Churchill happily orated that "'this was the crowning achievement of the long and glorious history of the British Secret Service'—or something like that."

Churchill's praise was for Juan Pujol Garcia, a Spanish spy who has been described as one of the most effective double agents in history. Working under the code name Garbo, Garcia convinced the Germans, who believed that he was their agent in London, that the Allied forces actually consisted of 75 divisions—in fact, there were 50 divisions—and that the remaining 25 divisions were about to be unleashed at the Pas de Calais, the narrowest point along the English Channel, almost 200 miles east of the actual landing site.

Whatever the long-term results, Garbo certainly helped defeat the Axis. He began his spying career as a freelance; he engaged the interest of the Abwehr, or German intelligence (after an initial rejection from the British secret services), and then settled in Lisbon, where he convinced the Germans that he had traveled to Britain and was setting up a network of spies. They paid him a total of 340,000 dollars over the course of the war to fund his imaginary network.

The British finally took him on in 1942 and moved him with his family to Britain.

Effective he may have been, but the greatest irony of Garbo's career was that he believed that by aiding the Allies, he would be hastening the end of dictator Francisco Franco's rule. Once World War II ended, Franco remained in power for 30 years.

GEORGE BLAKE

COLD WAR SPY

The first snow of the coming winter fell in occupied Berlin in late 1954. Near the border between the American and Soviet sectors, the snow drifted and blew and, along a straight line running into Russian-controlled territory, began to melt. The eye of an inquisitive Vopo, or East German policeman, might well have traced that line of slush back to a building in the American sector.

A horrified CIA officer looked out of the window at the melting snow and quickly gave a command to turn off the heat in the tunnel beneath the building. He heaved a sigh of relief.

On the East German side (we may speculate), a high-level counterpart to that CIA officer watched as the slush turned back to ice, soon covered with drifting snow, and chuckled to himself.

The Berlin Tunnel project—known as Operation Gold, implicitly a step up from Operation Silver, a similar cable-tapping, eavesdropping tunnel in Vienna—was blown by Blake even before a shovelful of dirt had been dug. After the joint American-British planning meeting where the decision was made to dig the tunnel, the junior British officer present, George Blake, was left behind to lock the documents in the safe. The occupying Soviet forces discovered the tunnel "accidentally," lest they reveal their source.

George Blake was born George Behne in 1922 to a Turkish Jewish father, naturalized as a British citizen, and a Dutch Lutheran mother, who named her son after the British king. In World War II Blake served in the Dutch resistance, the British navy, and MI6 (British foreign intelligence agency), and after the war was posted to Seoul. He was taken prisoner in 1950 when North Korean troops overran Seoul. During his imprisonment, the influence of a family member that

As a junior British intelligence officer, George Blake tipped off the Soviets about the Berlin Tunnel project, Operation Gold, before the first shovelful of dirt had been dug.

MI6 had failed to notice—his older cousin, a founding member of the Egyptian Communist Party—took hold, and Blake became a Russian agent. British intelligence took him back with open arms, and it was not until 1961 that a Polish defector tipped them off. Blake was tried and sentenced to 42 years in prison, one for each of the agents that had been executed as a result of his treason.

In 1966 the IRA helped Blake escape from Wormwood Scrubs prison, and he made his way to Moscow, where he still lives, enjoying "the happiest [years] of my life."

EXECUTED JULIUS AND ETHEL ROSENBERG

GUILTY as CHARGED

"It was a queer, sultry summer, the summer they electrocuted the Rosenbergs," reads the first half of the opening sentence of Sylvia Plath's The Bell Jar, a book that blazed a new path in fiction. "I couldn't help wondering what it would be like, being burned alive all along your nerves."

Sylvia Plath's obsession with the Rosenbergs and their 1953 execution was a strange, prurient, anxious interest, but it also reflected the massive impact that the trial for Soviet espionage of a Jewish, middle-class couple from Queens had on the American public, coming as it did less than ten years after the end of World War II and at the outbreak of the Korean War. Plath accurately reflects the massive publicity the trial and its aftermath received—"that's all there was to read about in the papers"—as well as the queasy feeling that the execution of a woman and a mother prompted in the American public.

The execution of Julius and Ethel Rosenberg struck a nerve. The names evoked by the execution of a woman were Mary Surratt, hanged for her marginal role in the assassination of Lincoln, and Ruth Snyder, electrocuted in Sing Sing for having conspired with her lover to murder her husband.

But Ethel Rosenberg was an unnervingly hapless figure, at least at first glance. At one point, when the prosecuting attorney was questioning her about a crucial piece of evidence against her and her husband, the photographic processing equipment found in their home upon their arrest, she responded, "I don't think I could

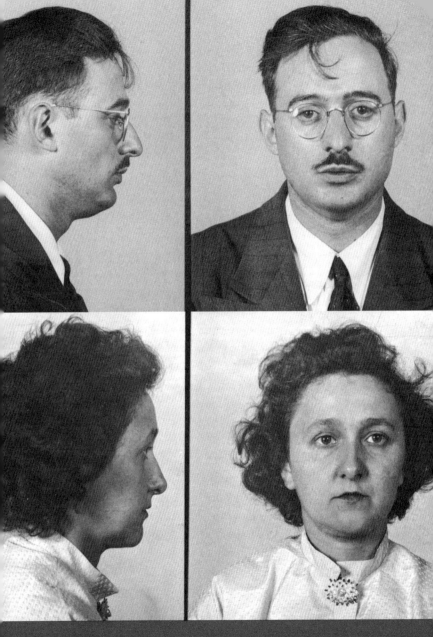

The Rosenbergs helped the Soviets acquire crucial A-bomb plans.

even describe it or name the stuff. It was just some developing developer, whatever you call it." A more endearingly noodle-headed Jewish-mother answer could not have been invented for her. She went on to point out that they were "snapshot hounds." Later, when it emerged that two halves of the same Jell-O box had been used as proof of identification in the Rosenberg case, she said that she had never heard of such a thing. The openly hostile judge, who ultimately sentenced both Rosenbergs to die, even though the Justice Department had asked that she be given a long prison term, then asked, "Incidentally, did you have any Jell-O boxes in your apartment?" "Oh, yes," Ethel Rosenberg replied.

Despite the unease, especially in left-wing political circles, about the execution of the Rosenbergs, strong evidence has emerged in more recent years pointing not only to his guilt, but her complicity. Intercepts of Soviet communications, code-named Venona and finally released in the mid-nineties, showed Soviet agents referring to Julius Rosenberg by the code names Liberal and Antenna, and reporting that Ethel Rosenberg knew "about her husband's work," although she did not "work" herself. The Russians also noted that she was a "devoted person," meaning that she espoused the Communist cause.

A brilliant critic named Robert Warshow was especially deft at skewering the flat, dutiful disingenuity of the Rosenbergs. He wrote, "On July 4, 1951, Julius clipped a copy of the Declaration of Independence from the New York Times and taped it to the wall of his cell. 'It is interesting,' he writes to Ethel, 'to read these words concerning free speech, freedom of the press and of religion in this setting. These rights our country's patriots died for can't be taken from the people even by Congress or the courts.' Does it matter that the Declaration of Independence says nothing about free speech, freedom of the press, or freedom of religion, and that Julius therefore could not have found it 'interesting' to read 'these words' in that particular document? It does not matter. Julius knew that America is supposed to have freedom of expression and that the Declaration of Independence 'stands for' America. Since, therefore, he already 'knew' the Declaration, there was no need for him to actually read it in order to find it 'interesting,' and it could not have occurred to him that he was being untruthful in implying that he had just been reading it when he had not. He could 'see himself' reading it, so to speak, and this dramatic image became reality: he did not know that he had not read it."

After all, the Rosenbergs weren't defending American freedoms. They had provided the Soviet Union with secrets that allowed it to develop the atomic bomb in the same arc of time in which North Korea—no friend of freedoms of any sort—was about to invade South Korea. The judge, who decided to inflict a penalty on Ethel more severe than the 30-years' imprisonment requested by the Department of Justice, said in his sentencing statement that the couple had "altered the course of history to the disadvantage of our country."

A further, disheartening aspect to the story was that the witness who did the most to ensure the couple's conviction was Ethel's brother, David Greenglass, also a member of the atomic spy ring.

In a surprising recent development, David Greenglass has admitted that the trial testimony provided by him and by his wife about the marginal role played by his sister in betraying atomic secrets to the Russians was perjured. Greenglass confessed, almost 50 years after his sister's execution, that the prosecution had pressured him, and that he had lied about Ethel typing secret information, so as to shield his wife from prosecution.

Philby was the most successful Soviet spy of the Cold War.

KIM PHILBY
& THE CAMBRIDGE SPY RING

The people in British intelligence might well have had some misgivings when Kim Philby, the head of a 30-man office in charge of sniffing out Soviet penetration agents, asked MI5, the British counterintelligence agency, to track down his ex-wife, Litzi Friedman, so he could obtain a divorce and be married to his prospective second wife. Philby's first wife was, in fact, living in East Berlin with a Soviet agent.

Apparently, however, the people at MI5 did not blink. But then, to have appointed Philby to head Section IX of the British foreign intelligence service, SIS, in the first place was, as he wrote later, "by anyone's standards a grotesque mistake to make."

But Philby was, as John le Carré later wrote, "an aggressive, upperclass enemy, [who] was of our blood and hunted with our pack; to the very end, he expected and received the indulgence owing to his moderation, good breeding and boyish, flirtatious charm."

If much of the explanation for how one of the most successful Soviet spies of the Cold War eluded detection for many years lies in the details of his birth into the British class system, the very reason he became a spy may well have to do with the father who sired him.

The father was named Harry Saint John Bridger Philby, but he went by Saint John; as his life progressed, he took other names, such as Abdullah, or Al Hajji. Saint John Philby was a dominating figure; an Arabist and an explorer, he was the first European to cross the Empty Quarter of Saudi Arabia from east to west. He replaced T. E. Lawrence (Lawrence of Arabia) as chief British representative in Trans-Jordan, but it was as a close adviser to Ibn-Saud and a pioneering businessman in the development of the Saudi oil industry that he made his mark.

Saint John Philby was a father that any boy would have worshiped, but Harold Adrian Russell Philby had to do his worshipping from a distance. If Saint John chose his own nickname, he also chose his son's: Kim, born in India, was a clear reference to the character from Kipling, to whom Allah gave "two separate sides to my head," and who learned to take part in the Great Game between England and Russia for control of India.

The two separate sides to Kim Philby's head were his role as a British intelligence officer and his much deeper allegiance, to a circle of Communist friends from university and, along with those friends, the ideal homeland of Soviet Russia.

It is important to remember what a shock the Great Depression caused in the insular and snobbish English college towns of Cambridge and Oxford. Before the early to mid-thirties, not only was left-wing politics absent from "Oxbridge," all politics was absent. The Depression led the college crowd to the belief that capitalism was teetering on its last legs.

This atmosphere produced what later became known as the Cambridge Spy Ring, a term conventionally used to describe five main agents: Kim Philby, Anthony Blunt, Guy Burgess, Donald Maclean, and John Cairncross. Another member of the group was probably Leo Long, a Cambridge student. But once investigations really got going, the tentacles of the group led to a much larger network of Soviet spies, as many as 40 agents, according to one account.

They were an odd crew: aesthetes, homosexuals, and members of England's hereditary, well-schooled elite.

The three most important members of the ring, Philby, Burgess, and Maclean all spent time on official missions in the United States, where they had access to American counterespionage efforts, sensitive nuclear intelligence, and military secrets.

They were spectacularly effective, producing so much useful intelligence that their Soviet handlers wondered at times if they weren't double agents, leading Russians by the nose. But they were real spies, working in earnest.

Even so, their abilities extended only so far. At one point, the Soviet handlers asked the flamboyantly gay Guy Burgess to court Winston Churchill's niece, Clarissa Churchill. As one pair of writers noted the results: he "made a feeble try."

Effective as they were, the group had some profoundly dysfunctional habits. Maclean was such an alcoholic that friends had dubbed his drunken alter ego "Gordon," after the boar on the label of the gin of that name. Often suffering from crippling hangovers, his hands trembled, his face was "usually a livid yellow and he looked as if he had spent the night sitting up in a tunnel," as a friend recalled.

Burgess, who was living with Philby's family at one point in Washington, came in drunk while the Philbys were at dinner with a number of high FBI and CIA officials, insulting the assembled guests and arousing intense suspicions.

And yet this very same reckless behavior could be harnessed to produce good spycraft. When it became clear that British counterintelligence was hot on their trail, Philby ordered Burgess to get himself recalled to London, where he could warn Maclean. A wild drive to South Carolina in his Lincoln convertible did the trick: Burgess racked up three speeding tickets and insulted several Virginia troopers on the way down to a diplomatic event at the Citadel in South Carolina.

Maclean and Burgess soon fled to Russia; Philby did not have to follow them for a good ten years. Lord Birkenhead wrote: "We shall never know how many agents were killed or tortured as a result of Philby's work as a double agent. He is now safe in Russia, and we must, alas, abandon any wistful dream of seeing this little carrion gibbeted."

EXECUTED
DIMITRI POLYAKOV

CROWN JEWEL OF U.S. INTELLIGENCE

Dimitri Polyakov, code name TOP HAT, is thought to have been the highest-ranking GRU (Soviet military intelligence) officer ever to spy for the West. He also appears to have had the unfortunate distinction of being betrayed by two Soviet spies: Aldrich Ames of the CIA and Robert Hanssen of the FBI.

Sandy Grimes of CIA counterintelligence, who helped to catch Ames, said of Polyakov that he "was our crown jewel, the best source …American intelligence has ever had. He worked for us for so many years and he achieved such a rank that…eventually we were able to look at…the GRU…from the top down…. The perspective certainly is a lot different when you're the CEO of a corporation than if you're the secretary in a middle manager's office."

Polyakov was a "walk-in," or volunteer spy. His first official contact was with the commanding general of the U.S. First Army (at his own request). To set the tone for what happened later, his second contact was with an FBI agent claiming to be a CIA officer.

Polyakov spied for the U.S. for almost 20 years, both from Moscow and then from various foreign capitals where he was posted as a military attaché. He seemed to be spying for his anti-Communist beliefs; Sandy Grimes said Polyakov was "very principled and he loved his country. He was a Russian first and foremost,…and he loved his people. What he didn't love was the leaders of his country."

As Polyakov moved up the ranks from lieutenant colonel to GRU general the scope of material that he could provide—ranging from Russian agents to military and intelligence secrets—expanded. Despite the doubts of counterintelligence chief James Jesus Angleton,

Polyakov had good reason not to want to be photographed.

the CIA ultimately decided that Polyakov was a genuine defector in place. And he paid the ultimate price. Following tip-offs from Ames and Hanssen, in 1986, six years after retiring, Polyakov was executed.

Sandy Grimes recalls: "I was devastated.... To lose him like this, when you were fairly confident that he had made it through, he had survived, he was retired, there was going to be a happy ending to this story, and when there wasn't, in some respects it was really more than you could bear."

PHAM XUAN AN

GENTLE SPY

Pham Xuan An fed information to the North Vietnamese while working as a stringer for *Time* magazine.

There is a famous photograph of the fall of Saigon: a helicopter perched atop a building, and people climbing a narrow ladder to board. It is regularly misidentified as being atop the U.S. Embassy, while it was actually the specially reinforced elevator shaft housing on top of the Pittman Apartments, where the CIA station chief and many CIA officers lived. And the photograph is often misremembered, with people dangling from the helicopter skids.

Instead, the evacuation is proceeding in an orderly manner, with a CIA officer helping people onto the single-blade Air America chopper. One of the last people to board is Tran Kim Tuyen, South Vietnam's spymaster. Not in the photograph, but reportedly waving goodbye from the sidelines, is Pham Xuan An, Time magazine's last reporter in Vietnam. He had arranged for Tuyen to escape, a singularly elegant gesture from a North Vietnamese spy who held the rank of colonel; after the war he was made a general and a Hero of the People's Armed Forces.

Pham worked, variously, for the French Deuxième Bureau, the CIA (under Edward Lansdale), the South Vietnamese intelligence organization, and its North Vietnamese counterpart. At one point he worked as a press censor for the Vietnamese post office, chopping and snipping bits of Graham Greene's dispatches to Europe.

Once he became a reporter for Time, he spent his nights typing up dispatches to Hanoi. They were run by courier to the tunnel network that was Communist headquarters, driven from there to Cambodia, flown to southern China, and then taken to the North Vietnamese Politburo, where General Giap and Ho Chi Minh eagerly read them.

Although the communists willingly accepted Pham's help, in the end he suffered the fate of all double agents: neither side really trusted him. At war's end he was about to immigrate to the U.S., but at the last minute, plans changed. He was detained in Hanoi and ordered to submit to reeducation.

VITALY YURCHENKO

DEFECTOR and RE-DEFECTOR

One evening in 1985, Vitaly Yurchenko stood up from a meal in a restaurant in the elegant Georgetown section of Washington, D.C., bid his CIA hosts goodnight, and—just like that—he was gone. Not physically gone. It was, shall we say, a slow and painful dissolve. In fact, the dust cloud caused by Yurchenko's disappearance has never quite settled.

Yurchenko's father died in World War II when he was a boy; the upward trajectory of his career moved him through the Soviet navy, into the KGB, and finally overseas in the late seventies. He was the chief of security for the Soviet Embassy in Washington, D.C., in the last half of the decade, and he liked to fraternize with his FBI counterparts, drinking scotch in an E Street restaurant called Dankers.

He was transferred back to Moscow and put in charge of domestic counterintelligence (where he regularly interacted with such Western defectors as George Blake and Kim Philby). After five years, his focus shifted back to Washington, with a prized new assignment: deputy chief, First Department, First Chief Directorate, KGB. Which meant that he was now in charge of KGB spying in North America.

Later he was stationed in Rome, and it was from there that he made a call from a pay phone, one day in August 1985, to the American Embassy. Soon afterward he defected to the West, ostensibly bringing with him one of the biggest intelligence hauls in recent years.

And soon he was indeed producing: He provided clues to two moles, Ronald Pelton in the NSA, and Edward Lee Howard, a former CIA employee. But opinions diverged sharply about the value of these two bags. Pelton might already have been considered to be a burned-out case, and Howard was never caught and managed to make his way

A year after reports of Yurchenko's execution—and a bill to his family for the cost of the bullets, in classic KGB style—he surfaced on a West German talk show, ebulliently denying his death.

to Moscow. The CIA, however, gloated over its trophy and debriefed him at length in an isolated house in the Maryland countryside.

Then, one rainy Saturday evening in November of that same year, in Au Pied de Cochon, an all-night eatery not particularly known for its food, Yurchenko stood up and reportedly said to his CIA escort, "If I'm not back in 15 minutes, don't blame yourself." He then left the restaurant—accounts vary, either walking out the front door, exiting through the kitchen, or climbing out a bathroom window. Then he walked about ten blocks to the Soviet compound, where he spent the rest of the weekend. On the following Monday he held a bizarre post-defection press conference, and days later a State Department psychologist confirmed that he was indeed re-defecting voluntarily.

He is now said to be working as a guard in a Russian bank, at close to age 70.

FEMME FATALES

SPIES IN A MAN'S WORLD

hen Napoleon Bonaparte said, "a spy in the right place is worth 20,000 soldiers on the battlefield," it may have sounded like an equal opportunity advertising pitch to women interested in patriotic glory and military derring-do. Of course, there is a downside to the equation, as Mata Hari learned to her intense discomfort: It is far easier to execute a spy than to kill 20,000 soldiers on the battlefield.

Easier, perhaps, but hardly gentlemanly. In the history of female spies, especially those who traded on charm, allure, and beauty, one of the chief tools of the trade was the creative twisting and crumpling of an age-old double standard. Gallantry, a somewhat block-headed old-fashioned military virtue, rested on an often blind assumption of modesty and purity. Even in the heart of the Civil War, Belle Boyd repeatedly received a courteous bow from her captors when a male spy in similar straits would have been hanged the next morning. And Josephine Baker, during World War II, swept glamorously past checkpoints, concealing documents beneath her fur coat.

APHRA BEHN

PUNK and POETESS

Aphra Behn, "poor shee-spye," spied for King Charles II in Amsterdam, but ended up in a debtor's prison for her efforts.

Aphra Behn was the first Englishwoman known to have earned a living by her pen. She was a prolific Restoration playwright, and sufficiently daring (one of her poems describes the "Hell of impotence") that she had detractors in her own time ("Punk and Poetess," one called her, basically identifying her as a streetwalker). Alexander Pope belittled her, and the Victorian era condemned her roundly. But before becoming a writer she had worked as a spy for King Charles II in Amsterdam, and possibly in Surinam (a new, sugar-producing English colony, formerly Dutch). It may even be that she traveled to Surinam at some point for purposes of spying.

Espionage, however, brought her only debt and danger; she warned the king that a Dutch fleet was going to blockade the Thames, and like so many spies before her (and after), she was ignored. Her warnings, however, had been easier to ignore than the actual Dutch fleet, which materialized threateningly in the Thames in 1667.

Other spies in Antwerp at the same time wrote scoffingly of the "poor shee-spye" who had managed to take up residence in a boardinghouse bristling with Dutch agents. Aphra wrote numerous pleading letters to the government, and was apparently finally reimbursed for the sizable debts she had incurred, but not before she was forced to sell jewelry and finally experience the social shame of "an execution"—debtor's prison.

Once she managed to extricate herself from debt—a process that involved a series of relatively well-to-do lovers—she entered the louche world of the theater, and resolved to make her living by writing. One of her most important creations was *Oroonoko*, considered one of the building blocks in the creation of the English novel. A play, *The Rover*, was set among British Cavaliers in Madrid and Naples during the exile of Charles II.

Virginia Woolf especially admired her, saying of the "shady and amorous" Aphra Behn that "all women together ought to let flowers fall upon [her] tomb, which is, most scandalously but rather appropriately, in Westminster Abbey, for it was she who earned them the right to speak their minds."

SARAH EDMONDS

CANADIAN CHAMELEON

Sarah Edmonds was a woman who pretended to be a man, a white who pretended to be a black slave, a Union soldier who pretended to be a Confederate, and—years after the Civil War ended—a Canadian who pretended that all her espionage was done out of her burning sense of American patriotism.

Before the war was even over, she wrote a book with a sensationalized title: Unsexed: or, The Female Soldier. The Thrilling Adventures, Experiences and Escapes of a Woman, as Nurse, Spy and Scout, in Hospitals, Camps and Battle-Fields. Unsurprisingly, the book sold well; remarkably, Edmonds—who was nothing if not authentic in her chameleon-like impersonations—accepted none of the profits, but donated them to veterans relief funds.

Five years after she arrived in the States the Civil War broke out, and Sarah cropped her hair, dressed in men's clothes, and enlisted in the Union Army under the alias Frank Thompson, serving at first as a male nurse. At the time, induction involved only answering a series of questions, and there was no physical examination.

She volunteered to serve as a spy (how much more complicated could it be?), and for her first mission used chemicals to darken her skin and a minstrel-show wig to disguise herself as a young African-American man, assuming the name Cuff.

Although she claimed to be a freeman, she was set to work building fortifications. She stayed behind Confederate lines for three days, learning valuable military plans, sketching the defenses, and counting guns (including "Quaker cannons," logs painted black to look like artillery). After a dozen missions, a case of malaria—and the danger of detection while under medical treatment—chased her out of the ranks.

...dmonds was the only female member of the Union veterans organization.

BELLE BOYD

LA BELLE REBELLE

After the battle, General Jackson wrote Boyd: "I thank you, for myself and for the army, for the immense service that you have rendered your country today."

Belle Boyd, known variously as the Cleopatra of the Secession and La Belle Rebelle, was said to be an impetuous and effective spy. Writers have painted her life in vivid colors, fascinated especially by the romantic aura surrounding a beautiful champion of a lost cause. One surviving document suggests that they may not have been exaggerating: the brash and determined letter she wrote President Abraham Lincoln from her exile in London. "I have heard…that if I suppress the Book…now ready for publication, you may be induced to consider leniently the case of my husband… I think it would be well for you & me to come to some definite understanding…. If you will release my husband…I pledge you my word that my Book shall be suppressed." The book in question detailed her "mistreatment" at Union hands. Closing the letter with "trusting an immediate reply," the most notorious Confederate spy launched yet another toss of the dice (this one, predictably, unsuccessful). And yet we can imagine the President reading this letter with a smile and a shake of the head, setting it aside for possible later action.

Born in Martinsburg, Virginia (later to become West Virginia, during the war), Belle was barely 18 when a Union soldier of the occupying forces tried to raise an American flag over her home. She promptly drew a pistol and shot him, and then wheedled her way out of the consequences with "tears and smiles."

So successful was her wheedling that, to the horror of the astonished town, she began to fraternize with Northern officers, flirting shamelessly and surreptitiously sending off notes to the Southern army of Stonewall Jackson and Jeb Stuart. But those notes were unenciphered, and when one was intercepted, she became a suspect. When a Union general commandeered her aunt's house, she took advantage of the opportunity. As a council of war was going on in the living room, Belle lay on the floor of an upstairs closet, her ear to a convenient knothole. That night she rode 15 miles, passing through Union lines with her passes, and returning before dawn.

Her most spectacular exploit, however, involved physical courage as well as nerve. Belle was in Front Royal when Stonewall Jackson's army moved against the town, and she learned that the occupying Union Army was planning to burn the bridges and block Jackson's advance. She ran through Union lines, cutting across open fields, her white apron an excellent target for soldiers on both sides. As she drew close to Confederate lines, she waved her bonnet as a sign to advance. The resulting Confederate victory prolonged the Civil War.

Mata Hari's history as a spy is obscured by her extravagant life.

EXECUTED

MATA HARI

THE EYE OF MORNING

Nothing could be more ambiguous than sex and espionage, nothing could be less ambiguous than death. Mata Hari brought all three together to stunning effect on the morning of October 15, 1917. Although it was the middle of World War I, a time when nearly 10,000 people—soldiers and civilians—were dying every day, the execution of a single woman continues to fascinate 90 years later.

One aspect of the scene was its grotesque whimsy. Mata Hari, dressed in a fashionable pearl-gray dress, silk stockings, stylish shoes, a corset, and a broad-brimmed straw hat, and courageously refusing a blindfold, actually waved and blew kisses at the 12-man firing squad as they took aim. None of her lovers, spymasters, or relatives claimed her body afterward, and it went to a medical school for dissection.

Mata Hari was born Margaretha Gertrud Zelle to a small-town Dutch hat-shop owner and his Javanese wife. In short order she was expelled from the school she was attending, after she was caught having sex with the headmaster, and married a captain named MacLeod in the Dutch colonial army. They moved to the Dutch East Indies, and she bore him two children, but they returned to Holland in 1905 and he abandoned her, taking the surviving daughter with him.

She made her way to Paris, calling herself at first Lady MacLeod and then Mata Hari, the "Eye of Morning." Soon she was performing as an exotic dancer, often quite nude, attracting enormous attention and taking lovers in the elevated ranks of society.

In 1917 the French and the British accused her of spying for the Germans; it is not clear that she ever did, and in any case one French officer may have been determined to justify the expense of having her trailed and closely watched by two men for six months.

VIRGINIA HALL

THE LIMPING LADY

Virginia Hall was named an MBE (Member of the British Empire) and received a Distinguished Service Cross for her work as an undercover agent in occupied France, helping to form the first OSS network in Vichy France.

And yet she might well have been proudest of an unofficial citation from the Gestapo in France. It did not even mention her name, but it did refer to her distinctive limp: "The woman who limps is one of the most dangerous Allied agents in France. We must find and destroy her." It accompanied a reasonably accurate sketch of her face.

Proud, but uneasy. This Gestapo wanted poster was being circulated before Virginia Hall returned to France for her second stint as an agent behind the lines (the first stint had been as agent for the British SOE—Special Operations Executive—before the U.S. entered the war).

Hall and her OSS handlers probably didn't know at the time that the Gestapo was looking for her, but she had been urged to modify her features radically. She refused that suggestion, but she did take on a new persona. She dyed her hair a dirty gray-black, and pulled it up severely with a wooden hairpin; she wore a special dress to make her look fatter; and she learned to walk with a swinging gait, to conceal her wooden leg, the result of a freak prewar hunting accident.

Her exploits in France were remarkable and numerous; her network of agents and partisans destroyed bridges and killed many Germans. But one description of her is especially eloquent. OSS agent Lt. René Julian Defourneaux recalled, "I was completely surprised at her appearance. She looked like an old lady with dark gray hair, dressed completely in black.... However, she still looked like a queen.... There was an alertness about her, as if she were still watching for an ambush."

Virginia Hall was a highly decorated Allied agent.

MATHILDE CARRÉ
LONE GAL TRIPLE AGENT

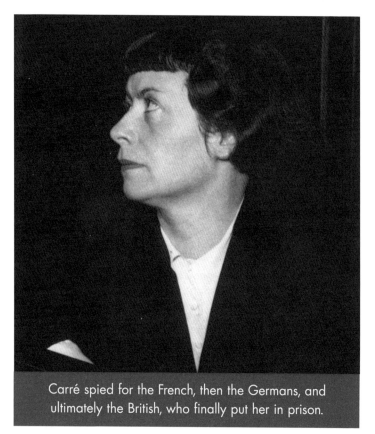

Carré spied for the French, then the Germans, and ultimately the British, who finally put her in prison.

Astrology may not be a reliable tool for espionage, but everyone who dealt with Mathilde Bélard Carré during her spying career might have been well advised to read her star chart. Born under Cancer, with Taurus rising: devious, with a strong survival instinct.

As the only known female triple agent in World War II, Carré was clearly a survivor. The daughter of a decorated French officer, she joined the Resistance in German-occupied Paris in 1940. Her underground code names were Lily and, later, Chatte (Cat).

When her network—the Interallié, run by Polish expatriates in France—was betrayed, Carré was arrested by the Germans in late 1941, along with 20 other agents. Carré was offered a deal, and she accepted, avoiding the firing squad but causing the arrest of about a hundred other members of the network. She accepted a salary of 60,000 francs a month, and helped to continue the radio transmissions to London, using the codes, schedules, and hidden security checks of Interallié. She was now a double agent.

Before the British became aware of the arrests, Carré was helping an SOE operative named Pierre de Vomecourt to escape from occupied France. When he became suspicious and confronted her, she began to cry and confessed all. Together they traveled back to England. There, Carré became a triple agent, divulging names of German officers and details of their counterintelligence activities.

When de Vomecourt returned to France and was captured by the Germans in April 1942, the British decided that the Germans might soon learn about the triple cross. Her usefulness as an agent was over, and she spent the rest of the war in a British prison. Handed over to the French in 1949, she was sentenced to death. Her sentence was commuted, and she was released in 1954, after 12 years behind bars.

In 1959 she wrote On m'appelait la chatte (They Called Me the Cat), and posthumously, Ma Conversion (My Conversion) was published, an account of how she became a Roman Catholic. Interestingly, for both books she chose to keep her code name, publishing as Lily Carré. Although spy novelist David Cornwell insists that his pen name John le Carré was suggested by a shop window sign, one has to wonder.

SPYCATCHERS

MASTERS OF COUNTERESPIONAGE

n the old *Mad* magazine of the sixties and seventies, there was a regular, wordless comic strip called *Spy vs. Spy*. Two identical spies, dressed symmetrically--one all in white, the other all in black--in broad-brimmed hats and dark sunglasses, would savage one another with reciprocally backfiring stunts and subterfuges.

Arguably the most baffling and psychically damaging field of espionage is that of the spycatcher, who works in what has been called the "wilderness of mirrors."

That memorabble phrase was coined by James Jesus Angleton, former chief of CIA counterintelligence, who is believed to have been forced into retirement because of his relentless--some thought obsessive--hunt for a mole who was never found. Peter Wright, head spycatcher for Great Britain, also engaged in a fruitless, years-long search for a highly placed mole.

The late J. Edgar Hoover was one of the longest-lived spycatchers that we know of: almost 50 years as the chief of the investigative branch of the U.S. Department of Justice. Whatever other personality traits he may have had, unbalancing paranoia does not seem to have been one of them. Richard Nixon called him a "pillar of strength in a city of weak men."

WILLIAM MELVILLE

BRITAIN'S FIRST SPYCATCHER

Melville may have been the model for Ian Fleming's "M."

If "Ace of Spies" Sidney Reilly (actually a Russian-born Jew named Sigmund Rosenblum) was the model for James Bond, new evidence suggests that William Melville might have been the basis for "M."

Many others had been posited as Ian Fleming's monogrammatic spymaster, but a new book by Andrew Cook argues that it was Melville. Whoever inspired "M," Melville led an astonishing life. Born in rural Ireland in 1850, the son of a pubowner and baker, Melville joined the London police force at 22, and was made a member of the new and elite Special Irish Branch ten years later, to deal with a wave of Irish separist bombings, including an attempt to destroy Nelson's Column.

In time, SIB mutated into the Special Branch, a sort of British secret service. Over the course of his career, Melville thwarted an attempt on Queen Victoria's life, helped to secure British control of Persia's oil resources—fundamental to fueling navy warships in World War I, and to the foundation of BP, one of the world's largest companies—helped to infiltrate Russian anarchist groups in London (where Sidney Reilly was one of his agents), and tracked the movements of one of the chief suspects in the Whitehall Murders (better known as the Jack the Ripper killings).

In late 1903 Melville resigned his post and ostensibly established a small private detective agency. Cook claims—though some historians dispute this interpretation of events—that in fact Melville had become Britain's first official spymaster (rather than the official first heads of MI6 and MI5, Sir Mansfield Cumming and Vernon Kell, respectively "C" and "K").

Whatever the true story of Melville's years of operating under the alias of Morgan (ostensible owner of the small detective agency), there is another strong candidate for the model of "M." Apparently that was Ian Fleming's nickname for his stern and redoubtable mother.

FELIKS DZERZHINSKY

FOUNDER OF THE CHEKA

Feliks Dzerzhinsky, Catholic and Polish-born in 1877, at first wanted to become a priest. Increasingly involved in revolutionary politics and the overthrow of the czarist state, he founded the Soviet Cheka, a secret police tasked to combat counterrevolution, trading the administration of religious confessions for the relentless pursuit of another sort—and often dispensing with confessions entirely.

He may have abandoned his youthful dreams of priesthood, but as a boy in Russian-occupied Poland he fantasized about owning a magic cap that would, in his own words, allow him "to slay all the Russians." Early in his career as the head of the first Soviet secret police organization, it must have seemed as if he had found that magical cap.

Dzerzhinsky spent much of the run-up to the October 1917 revolution in prison, but as soon as he was freed, he allied himself with the Bolsheviks and was soon a recognized leader. He was dubbed "Iron Feliks" for his hard work, long hours, and uncompromising attitude toward dissidents.

The Cheka (an acronym, actually short for Vecheka, that stood for "Extraordinary Commission," or in its full version, "All-Russian Extraordinary Commission for Combating Counterrevolution, Speculation, Sabotage and Misconduct in Office") was one of the first Bolshevik institutions, founded before the end of 1917.

The Cheka was fairly restrained in its use of terror until late August 1918. Its ferocity was aroused when British, French, and American agents were arrested in one of the opening incidents of the counterrevolutionary civil war, and an attempt was made on Lenin's life. By the end of the civil war, 200,000 Russians had been executed,

"Iron Feliks" created a huge machine for repression.

and the Cheka had swollen—by mid-1921—to an organization of a quarter million people, from its original size of just a few hundred.

Dzerzhinsky collapsed in 1926 in the middle of a heated argument with Stalin: either a victim of the strain of his years in prison, or of nefarious methods that he himself had helped to pioneer.

J. EDGAR HOOVER

THE ORIGINAL G-MAN

A glance around the magnificent main reading room of the Library of Congress offers a glimpse of one of the great collections of books on Earth. Magnificent as this collection may be in purely intellectual terms, it has a practical purpose indicated by the name. This library is for the use of men and women with political aims, legislators who hold immense power.

In the early years of the past century, one of the file clerks working in the Library of Congress may have taken special note as he sensed this direct relationship between information and power. His name was John Hoover. John Edgar Hoover.

His education complete—a bachelor's and a master's degree in law—Hoover took a clerk's job at the Department of Justice, fortuitously in the section responsible for the registration of enemy aliens, just as the United States was about to enter World War I. In a neighboring office, holding the title of "alien property custodian," was a man named A. Mitchell Palmer. Two years later, in 1919, President Woodrow Wilson appointed Palmer attorney general, and Hoover soon became Palmer's special assistant.

Palmer took advantage of new legislation—the Espionage Act of 1917 and the Sedition Act of 1918—to unleash the infamous Red Scare, in the atmosphere of panic prompted by the Bolshevik Revolution of 1917.

The numbers are astonishing. Hoover quickly accumulated files on 200,000 people and organizations, and ordered the arrest of over 200 members of a Russian labor union; about a month later, in January 1920, Hoover ordered the arrest of about 10,000 people in 33 cities, detaining them at length.

Hoover understood that information was power and used it effectively.

In 1924, in the wake of the disastrous and corruption-riddled administration of Warren G. Harding, Hoover was appointed director of the Justice Department's Bureau of Investigation, before he was 30.

As America turned inward, Hoover's bureau focused on criminals instead of subversives. He was an adroit manipulator of publicity, and the popularization of terms like G-man and collaboration with the film industry and other media attracted growing attention. One such project was G-Men, starring James Cagney.

Indicative of the focus on crime was the origin of the term G-man (G for government) as a specific reference to Hoover's bureau. It had originally been used to describe any federal agent, but in a kidnapping case that captured the national imagination—the Urschel case, which was solved in part by such clues as planes that flew twice daily over the remote hideout where the kidnapped man was held captive—a badly hung-over George "Machine Gun" Kelly called out to the bureau agents, "Don't shoot, G-men!"

In 1935 the agency was given its familiar title of the Federal Bureau of Investigation, with initials that Hoover, the canny image-maker, immediately recast as standing for "Fidelity, Bravery, Integrity."

Despite the focus on domestic crime and the creation of a G-man mystique, Hoover continued to keep a sharp eye on the shifting political stage. And he met a political animal he could work with in Franklin Delano Roosevelt. Then-Attorney General Francis Biddle recalled, "The two men liked and understood each other."

But Hoover's personal likes and dislikes spoiled what could have been a spectacular intelligence coup early in the war, even before the Americans became involved.

In the late summer of 1941 the British intelligence services introduced the FBI to Dusko Popov, a Yugoslavian playboy who was working as a double agent for them and the Germans. Among the information that his German masters had asked him to obtain was a small section on Pearl Harbor. Rightly or wrongly, it has been claimed that Hoover failed to see the value of Popov's information and did not pass it on to Roosevelt; Joseph Persico writes that not only was Hoover offended by Popov's activity as a playboy, but "Popov had dared stray into Hoover's favored night spot, the Stork Club."

Hoover effectively sat on this information. Hindsight made it the only piece of prior intelligence pointing to the impending Japanese sneak attack; in reality the Germans were as surprised by the Japanese raid as anyone. Hoover might have refused to dirty his hands with a "Balkan playboy" like Popov, but he moved quickly after the attack on Pearl Harbor. Within three days of the declaration of war, the FBI had rounded up more than 2,000 Japanese, German, and Italian aliens.

He met with—and refused to deal with—representatives from the British secret services, one of whom was Ian Fleming, later the creator of James Bond. Ian Fleming recalled Hoover: "A chunky, enigmatic man with slow eyes and a trap of a mouth.... His negative response was as soft as a cat's paw."

After the war, Hoover's chief legacy in the area of intelligence was in part tainted by his snooping on alleged Communists and on activists of all sorts. Those who depended on him appreciated especially his familiarity with the levers of power, and information, of course, is power. Lyndon Johnson told his successor, Richard Nixon, that Hoover was a crucial player in the capital. Memorably, he said, "He is a pillar of strength in a city of weak men."

It was not until after his death that rumors began to surface of his homosexuality, along with jokes to the effect that "J. Edgar Hoover was certainly the toughest lawman ever to wear a dress."

JAMES JESUS ANGLETON

WILDERNESS OF MIRRORS

CIA chief of counterintelligence James Jesus Angleton, who was such an integral part of the agency's history that at one point it was proposed that his lean, angular profile be used in the CIA logo, famously described counterespionage as a "wilderness of mirrors."

The phrase has been identified with him at least in part because of his relentless—some thought even obsessive—hunt for a Soviet mole in the agency. In 1974 CIA director William Colby forced him to resign in order to put a stop to the hunt. The phrase has come to describe an intricate puzzle palace that can drive anyone over the edge.

Though many believe that Angleton made up the phrase himself, it was in fact a quote from T. S. Eliot's "Gerontion." In the same poem, reference is made to "a thousand small deliberations," and the poet asks: "will the spider…suspend its operations?" All are phrases evocative of Angleton's future career.

Angleton was a lover of poetry, and was in fact a co-founder—while a student at Yale—of an estimable little poetry magazine called Furioso. One of his mentors in this enterprise was none other than the great poet Ezra Pound, who wrote at one point that he was glad to offer advice in his capacity of "padre eterno or whatever," using the Italian phrase for "Almighty God." Since Ezra Pound was later arrested in Italy for having made anti-American broadcasts for the Fascists, and was then declared "insane and mentally unfit for trial," and held for 12 years in an insane asylum, this early mentor provides an unsettling leitmotiv for Angleton's later obsession.

The name of Angleton's poetry magazine provides another haunting clue: Furioso is in fact a clear reference to Ludovico Ariosto's

Angleton was forced to leave the CIA because of his incessant mole hunting.

"Orlando Furioso," an epic poem written during the Italian Renaissance, featuring a magical palace in which each warrior would chase endlessly after his heart's fondest desire. "Atlante's magic castle" proved ultimately to be as "insubstantial as thin air," and sadly, that was the judgment of Angleton's superiors upon his hunt for the elusive mole.

But a case may fairly be made that both Aldrich Ames and Robert Hanssen fit the bill of what Angleton was seeking.

Angleton was a refined man, and his love of poetry was matched by a fondness for fly fishing and for growing orchids as well as a love of good food and wine. His nicknames included Mother (for his seniority), the Gray Ghost (for his general appearance and style), and Virginia Slim (for his build and his favorite brand of cigarette). He had a romantic lineage: His father, Hugh Angleton, was a cavalry officer in the Idaho National Guard, who, when on a raid across the Mexican border during the career of Pancho Villa, met and married a 17-year-old Mexican beauty, Angleton's mother..

When James Jesus Angleton was a young man, his family moved from Boise, Idaho, to Rome, Italy, where his father worked as a representative for the National Cash Register company.

He attended an exclusive English private school and went back to the United States for college, at Yale.

A notice enclosed with the fourth issue of Furioso informed subscribers that "at least half our editorial board (one of us) is to be drafted. Just how much poetry will be...accepted, rejected in Camp So-and-So is a bitter question with a doubtful question mark." And in fact, both of the magazine's editors saw service, and only one issue appeared between 1941 and the end of World War II.

In 1943 Angleton joined the OSS. After a short period in London (where he paid visits to T. S. Eliot), he was sent to Rome, where he was put in charge of counterintelligence. One of the most important cases that he worked on in Rome, among the thousands of counter-intelligence cases that fell under his purview, involved an odd array of characters: Pope Pius XII; the pope's undersecretary of state, Giovanni Battista Montini (the future pope Paul VI); the Vatican's apostolic delegate to Tokyo; and a two-bit fraud and former author of risqué literature named Virgilio Scattolini.

Scattolini was the brother-in-law of the OSS chief of station in Rome, Victor Scamporini. His checkered career as an author included pro-German propaganda at the outbreak of World War I, a variety of steamy novels (*Trembling, She Kissed My Lips; Giannetta the Lovely Aviatrix;* and *The Girl of the Seven Sins*), and one novel entitled, revealingly, *The Art of Deceiving Your Fellow Man.* It would have been enough to check the catalog under his name at the Italian central library in Florence.

Instead, Scattolini's accounts of papal audiences with discussions of Russian plans for a separate peace with Japan were served up as genuine intelligence in briefings to President Franklin Roosevelt himself.

After Scattolini had been unmasked, Angleton, characteristically, kept him on the payroll (and completely in the dark) as if nothing had happened and continued to accept his reports.

Angleton went on to have a long and influential career in the CIA, a career that reached a crescendo of some sort with the baffling defection of Yuri Nosenko, a KGB officer—who had been, incidentally, Lee Harvey Oswald's case officer during his defection to Russia—whom Angleton suspected of being a deception agent.

Angleton arranged for Nosenko to be held as a captive of the CIA for four full years under grueling conditions. His case remained emblematic of Angleton's working methods, with suspicion elevated to a fine, and almost unbalanced, art.

MI5 was not particularly grateful to Wright for his spy-catching efforts.

PETER WRIGHT

MILLIONAIRE SPYCATCHER

Peter Wright was the first scientist hired by MI5, the British counter-intelligence agency. He figured out the mechanism of a Soviet bug concealed in the wooden replica of the Great Seal given by the Soviets in 1946 as a "housewarming" gift for the new American ambassador's residence in Moscow. He was the head of a major counterintelligence effort code named the Fluency Committee. And he died a millionaire.

All this might suggest that he was on good terms with his employer when he retired. But that was not the case at all.

Indeed, if Peter Wright died wealthy, it was despite the strenuous efforts to block the source of his wealth, the publication of a book entitled Spycatcher. In that book, Wright set forth some of the theories he had developed as a counterintelligence officer. One of his theories was that Sir Roger Hollis, the head of MI5 from 1956 until 1965, was a Soviet mole, the notorious suspected "fifth man" in the Cambridge Spy Ring of Kim Philby.

At one point, Furnival Jones, the head of MI5, wrote him: "Where's this going to end, Peter—you've sent me a paper which says that my predecessor and most likely my successor are both spies. Have you thought this through?" A government investigation found that Hollis had not been a spy. Wright also alleged that Prime Minister Harold Wilson was the target of a supposed MI5 conspiracy.

In 1988 the British government was finally defeated in its long-running fight to block the publication of Wright's book. Publication in England had become a moot question: Wright had circumvented any restrictions by publishing his book in Australia. It became a huge international best-seller, with millions of copies sold. It is not clear whether the book helped anyone but its author and publisher.

MASTERS OF TRADECRAFT

TRICKS OF THE TRADE

Spies go to work with a rich and varied bag of tricks and tools. Two of the most important tools of espionage are eavesdropping and code breaking, and one of the most interesting chapters in their history came in World War II. A subset of what is known as sigint (short for signals intelligence), code breaking certainly provided considerable help to both sides in the war. Early in the war, American code breakers knew that the Japanese were planning an attack on an American island outpost in the Pacific, but were uncertain about which one, because the name of the island was further concealed in an unbreakable internal code. They sent out a false message in an uncoded radio broadcast, saying that the garrison of Midway was running out of water, and a day later saw that same message referring to the mystery island. That knowledge was crucial in the victory of Midway.

But, as David Kahn quotes the head of U.S. Army code breakers, "If you try to estimate by how long code breaking shortened the war, you'd have the quartermaster claiming so many years, the air force so many, and everybody claiming some, and before you know it you'd find the war should have been over 25 years before it began!"

SIR WILLIAM REGINALD HALL

GETTING THE U.S. OFF THE SIDELINES

Hall, right, drew the U.S. out of isolationism and into WWI by sharing a telegram about Mexico invading the Southwest.

The nickname "Blinker" would seem to be a natural one for a DNI, or director of naval intelligence (in turn, the son of the first DNI), in Britain, where signal lamps had been used for nighttime communications in the fleet that guarded and administered an empire. But the reference was not to signals or intelligence: it was to the fact that

Hon. Adm. Sir William Reginald Hall's eyes had a tendency to blink repeatedly when he was excited.

The excitement could be contagious: as in 1918, when Blinker Hall, DNI during World War I welcomed Franklin D. Roosevelt, the new assistant secretary of the U.S. Navy, to his office. He introduced him to a young man who claimed to have just come fresh from behind enemy lines. It was, in fact, a ruse, but FDR told it as a true story a quarter century later, still under the spell of "Blinker" and the British navy.

Hall obtained excellent information from signals intelligence throughout the war. Chance—a stranded German warship and a lead box dredged up by a British trawler—brought Room 40, as the code breakers' office was known, the keys to several key German codes.

Unfortunately, the intelligence produced by Room 40 was not passed on when it was needed most. Naval incompetence on the day of the Battle of Jutland left crucial intelligence unutilized. As a result, the unprepared British navy suffered tremendous losses in that battle.

Not so later in the war, with the notorious "Zimmerman Telegram"—a note from German Foreign Secretary Arthur Zimmerman proposing a secret anti-American alliance to neutral Mexico in early 1917. Room 40 intercepted and decoded the telegram, and Hall placed the intelligence exactly where it was most useful, handing it over to the American State Department, whence it soon made its way into screaming headlines in newspapers across the nation: "Germany Seeks an Alliance Against U.S." and "German Plot to Conquer United States with Aid of Japan and Mexico Revealed."

The British couldn't have invented a better way to get the isolationists off the sidelines than to reveal a plan to hand New Mexico, Arizona, and Texas back to Mexico—a few weeks later the U.S. declared war on Germany. Hall must have been blinking in excitement.

HERBERT O. YARDLEY

NOT A GENTLEMAN

Indiana-born Herbert Yardley, according to a recent CIA book review, was "a precocious small-town boy on the make," who parlayed a State Department job as a telegrapher and an amateur's interest in code breaking into a critical role in the foundation of America's first permanent code-breaking institution: MI8 (the initials stand for "military intelligence"), which was very much the forerunner of the NSA.

If Yardley was there at the creation, his genius was too idiosyncratic and improvisational to keep him in place long. His great rival was William Friedman, who actually headed the organization out of which the NSA later developed. But Yardley led a very interesting life; David Kahn, the foremost expert on cryptanalysis, calls him "the most colorful and controversial figure in American intelligence."

His greatest cryptanalytical achievement was breaking the Japanese diplomatic code, offering the American negotiating team at the 1921 conference on limiting naval armaments a huge tactical advantage in a field that was crucial in the Second World War.

Yardley's triumph had a second, indirect effect that was subtle but crucial to American victory in the coming war. By breaking the hand-enciphered codes, Yardley forced the Japanese to adopt machine codes early, giving the Americans greater lead time to break them. Had the Japanese waited till later to switch to machine codes, the Americans might not have broken them until much later in the war. The crucial Battle of Midway might have gone differently.

But in 1929 Secretary of State Henry Stimson shut down Yardley's Cipher Bureau, justifying the action later with the notoriously prim observation that "gentlemen do not read each other's mail."

Yardley formed the first U.S. code-breaking institution, MI8, the forerunner of the NSA. His efforts were cut short by Secretary of State Henry Stimson, who believed that "gentlemen do not read each other's mail."

Yardley understandably rebelled against this prudish approach to the life-and-death business of intelligence; the form that his rebellion took made him a pariah, though a best-selling one.

He wrote a book about the Cipher Bureau entitled *The American Black Chamber.* He claimed that he had done so in order to call attention to America's shortcomings in code breaking; in response Congress banned a sequel, the only time that it has actually blocked the publication of a book. Yardley's other best-seller was a book on how to play poker, still widely read and considered a classic.

Turing was a brilliant cryptologist with an early vision of the binary comput

ALAN TURING

ENIGMA CODE BREAKER

Alan Mathison Turing is widely considered to have been one of the founders of computer science. He was also a crucial member of the British team at Bletchley Park, a top-secret facility in the English countryside, which was racing to break German codes encrypted through the Enigma machines.

It is difficult to identify the significance of Turing's bizarre method for killing himself, in 1954, at the age of 42. What appears to have happened is that Turing ate a cyanide-laced apple (though vague suspicions of skullduggery have continued to swirl). Could he have been paying grim tribute to another great British genius linked to an apple, Sir Isaac Newton? Perhaps. Turing, who was gay, might have been emulating another iconic figure, Disney's Snow White. Apparently he often cited the words of the Wicked Witch (let's not forget: actually an Evil Queen in disguise): "Dip the apple in the brew/Let the sleeping death seep through." Another, more rational, suggestion is that the apple offered plausible deniability: Turing's aged mother did console herself with the belief that her son had accidentally ingested a poisoned piece of fruit.

One of the foremost chroniclers of cryptology, David Kahn, describes him vividly:

"Alan Turing was a prodigy, a genius. A tallish, dark-haired, powerfully built man of twenty-seven with sunken cheeks and deep-set blue eyes, he wore unpressed clothes, picked at the flesh around his fingernails until it bled, stammered, fell into long silences, rarely made eye contact, sidled through doors, and ran long-distance races."

He received his Ph.D. from Princeton University in 1938 for his work on the "Decision Problem," a basic element of the developing field of computability and probability. One of his early theorizations was an endless tape marked into squares, and a machine that could read and change—or leave unchanged—each square, leaving it either marked or blank. This is the basic conceptual model of a binary computer.

At the outbreak of war, in the fall of 1939, Turing was already at work in Bletchley Park. The focus of his work, and that of much of Bletchley Park, was the German Enigma machine.

The original Enigma was developed as a business-coding machine. It used electrical circuits to create a randomly generated, nonrepeating code; another Enigma machine on the receiving side was used to decode the messages. During the war, the German armed forces used the Enigma machine to code their communications.

Just before the war the Polish intelligence services, with help from the French, were making great strides toward routinely breaking German codes with replicas of the Enigma machine that they had developed. They smuggled one of these out of Poland and into France just after the German invasion; it in turn was taken to Britain before the fall of France.

At Bletchley Park the code breakers, with Turing playing a leading role, developed a "bombe," code named the Bronze Goddess. The bombe—the name came either from its ominous ticking sound or, weirdly, from a Polish word for ice cream—was "a large copper-coloured cupboard" that contained the forerunner of an early computer.

Turing had helped to pave the way for the effort to develop the Colossus, which solved German high-command encrypted teletype-writer messages, using electronic processing, an important step toward the world's first computer.

Thanks to his efforts, and those of the larger team at Bletchley Park, the British and the Americans were able to break many coded German messages throughout the war.

Despite this success, Turing's personal life caused trouble. He was transferred to work on a voice scrambler in a different part of England in 1944 after reports were received of schoolboys being molested in a small town neighboring Bletchley Park.

At war's end, he was awarded the MBE—becoming an officer of the Order of the British Empire—for his work.

He did further pioneering work in the development of electronic digital computers. He was elected a fellow of the Royal Society in 1951, but things went downhill from there pretty quickly.

The following March, his male lover and an accomplice broke into Turing's house. Turing reported the burglary to the police; the investigation led to charges that Turing had had a sexual relationship with another man. Homosexuality was against the law at the time in Great Britain, and Turing was indicted for "gross indecency and sexual perversion," convicted, and sentenced to hormone treatments, which produced grotesque side effects, including the development of breasts.

One of the last areas of research in which Turing engaged, prior to his suicide, was the field of artificial intelligence. One of his contributions to the question of how to establish the existence of artificial intelligence was the so-called Turing Test. In order to determine whether a machine thinks, Turing said, as paraphrased by the Encyclopaedia Britannica: "A remote human interrogator, within a fixed time frame, must distinguish between a computer and a human subject based on their replies to various questions posed by the interrogator. By means of a series of such tests, a computer's success at 'thinking' can be measured by its probability of being misidentified as the human subject."

There is a website that offers a number of sample questions to ask such a hypothetical computer, and one of the questions might have amused Turing in particular. It asked, "If you are a human being and I guess you are a computer, have I failed the Turing test?"

LEON THEREMIN

GOOD VIBRATIONS

Although you might not think that Leon Theremin and Ben Franklin would really have that much in common, were they to meet on the astral plane or in some nondenominational afterlife that admitted Communists and spies, they actually would have a lot to talk about.

For instance, they both invented musical instruments that produce an ethereal, almost spooky sound: Franklin devised the glass harmonica; Leon Theremin invented the etherophone, later renamed the theremin, in honor of its inventor. But Ben Franklin's glass harmonica was never used by the Beach Boys; the theremin was.

And they were both spies. Franklin's life in espionage is discussed at some length in this book; Theremin's scaled the heights and plumbed the depths of the shadow world in Soviet Russia. Theremin spent time in a Siberian labor camp on trumped-up charges; he was also awarded the Stalin Prize for his invention of a miniature eavesdropping device used by the KGB. One of his most notorious inventions was a bug that was placed in the wooden replica of the Great Seal of the United States presented by a group of Russian schoolchildren to the American ambassador, Averell Harriman, in 1945. It was not until 1952 that the bug was discovered. The bug required no internal power source; a UHF beam from a nearby van activated it, and it modulated the beam that it reflected back to echo conversations in the room: Ambassador Harriman's residential office in Moscow.

Theremin immigrated to America in the aftermath of the Bolshevik Revolution and seemed to have preferred life in the United States. In fact, it is thought that he returned to the U.S.S.R. only because he was forcibly hustled out of the country by Soviet secret agents.

theremin was used in one of the Beach Boys' big hits, "Good Vibrations."

ANTONIO MENDEZ

MASTER OF DISGUISES

Mendez created a fake location-scouting company that could get into and out of Tehran with the six embassy staffers.

The news of a pioneering face transplant performed in France, recent as this book went to press anyway, was heralded with interest around the world. But Antonio J. Mendez and his many unidentified professional colleagues probably listened to the reports with a calm, measured interest distant from that of most. As they took notes and considered the logistical issue, they were probably pondering whether or not face-transplantation should be included in their bag of tricks.

That bag of tricks—such that Mendez is often compared to Ian Fleming's fictional master of disguise and gadgets, Q—included such items as "pocket litter," the kind of convincing bits of paper and detritus that will emerge in a thorough personal search.

These are fundamental subjects for people like Mendez—once a chief of disguise for the CIA; his wife succeeded him in the job.

Unquestionably the best known project in Mendez's career was the exfiltration of six embassy staff members from Tehran during the 1979 hostage crisis.

Although Mendez describes spending the first days of the hostage crisis on a diversionary plan—"I had already spent the first days of the crisis creating a deception operation designed to defuse the crisis. President Carter decided not to use this plan, however. He has since lamented that decision"—he was soon tasked with finding a way of extracting six Tehran Embassy employees who had not been caught by the hostage-takers and had secretly taken refuge at the Canadian Embassy.

It is commonplace in the movie industry to use show-business expedients as plot devices in the movies. Thus, you will often find that the solutions to problems in thrillers involve disguise, or stagecraft, or the sort of diversions that directors usually use. In this case, life imitated art. Mendez came up with the idea of creating a bogus location-scouting team that could leave Iran after exploring it as a site for the filming of a major motion picture.

Mendez called upon his contacts in the movie business, especially a makeup consultant he describes under the alias of "Jerome Callaway." Jerome suggested that a location-scouting crew would probably consist of about eight people, the perfect number. He quickly arranged for the CIA team to have an office on the Columbia Studios lot (it had just been vacated by Michael Douglas, who had used it while he was producing *The China Syndrome*). Jerome's involvement in the production gave it cachet; in fact, the CIA operatives did their best to keep Jerome's involvement a secret, but that is virtually impossible in Hollywood, and their very efforts to keep his involvement a secret gave the project even more cachet.

They called the production company "Studio Six Productions" (a reference to the six Americans), and decided to name the movie Argo. The title was a reference to classical antiquity, at least in appearance (and they chose to allow that reference to stand, at least in part because it was compatible with a project glorifying classical Islam), but in point of fact it was a veiled but very pointed insult. It is part of the punch line of a profane knock-knock joke that culminates, to put it euphemistically, Argo soak your head.

The development of the project sounds in many ways like the plot of Mel Brooks's The Producers. They chose one script because no one could figure out what the plot meant; the intricacy of the science-fiction story was beyond critical understanding.

They took out full-page ads for the production in Variety and the Hollywood Reporter. And on the strength of their feigned production deal, Mendez and another CIA operative traveled into Iran. What they found there was not as dire as one might have expected. The six "houseguests" of the Canadian ambassador were living well. They had been cooking gourmet meals in the professionally equipped kitchen, they had become quite expert Scrabble players, and when they learned that they were going to leave the country disguised as a film production team, they began to blow-dry their hair, sport gold medallions and open-neck shirts, and wear pocketless, tight-fitting trousers. It was a time of bad fashion, but it was all part of the plot. And just to keep a sense of the real dangers that were facing them, various journalists back in the West were beginning to notice that the number of hostages seized in the American Embassy compound and the number of embassy personnel released by the government were not matching up

Mendez disguised himself as a groovy Hollywood location scout in part of the operation to exfiltrate six embassy staff holed up in the Canadian Embassy in Tehran.

precisely. Moreover, in the Canadian compound, the sound of paper shredders and one particularly vigorous employee wielding a 12-pound sledgehammer to destroy sensitive telecommunications equipment was enough to keep things tense.

But the exfiltration went well. One sign of imminent success was the name on the nose of the Swissair flight that took the six out of the country: Argau, the name of a Swiss canton—close enough to Argo to augur freedom.

The final cable from the Canadian government to the embassy, approving the exfiltration plan, included the salutation: "See you later, exfiltrator."

When they returned to the United States, the CIA operatives learned that their production company had received several dozen script submissions in their absence, including one from Steven Spielberg.

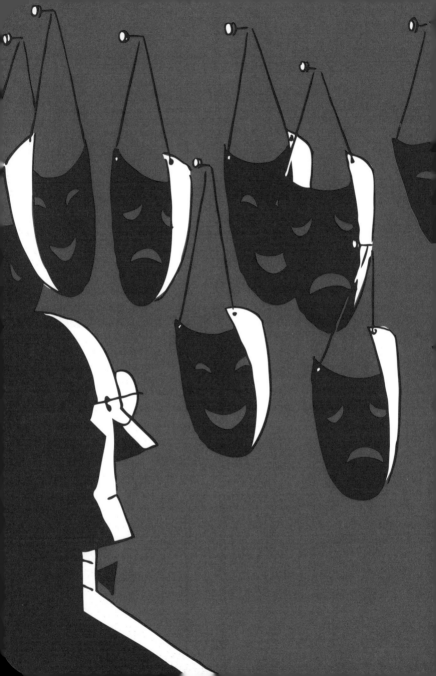

MASKS OF CELEBRITY

FAMOUS SPIES

Sometimes celebrity and spylike stealth are incongruous. One star reported to have been a spy (in Mexico, prior to America's entry into World War II) was Eddie Albert, best known for his role as Oliver Wendell Douglas on *Green Acres*. But, as befits a spy, Albert's mild persona was misleading: He won a Bronze Star (with combat "V") for rescuing 70 Marines during the savage Battle of Tarawa. And he won an Oscar for his acting in *Roman Holiday*, and played opposite Ronald Reagan in *Brother Rat*. So there's a wilderness of mirrors even in show business.

One of the best known celebrity spies was Josephine Baker; it is easy to imagine her, a French citizen in Vichy France, sweeping through customs with a panther on a leash and secret plans hidden in her undergarments; equally evocative is the figure of Sterling Hayden, a hard-drinking spectacularly handsome movie star who considered his time in the OSS to have been the best years of his life.

SWASHBUCKLING PLAYBOY

Rogue and inventor, Beaumarchais considered himself the savior of the American Revolution.

Pierre Caron de Beaumarchais lived a life as giddy and exciting as any imaginary James Bond, but was a literary genius as well as a secret agent. He was a successful businessman, adroit courtier, and skilled publicist, as well as considering himself—with some justification—the savior of the American Revolution.

He first gained the attention of the French court by inventing an escapement that made it possible to make very slim, flat watches; he made a watch for Madame de Pompadour so small that it fit into her ring. He further consolidated his entry into the French court by purchasing—or wheedling—the position of waiter at the king's table from an elderly noble. When the noble died, he married the widow and inherited the landholding and title of Beaumarchais.

Another invention of his, improving the placement of the foot pedals on the harp, brought him to the notice of King Louis XV's unmarried daughters. His rocketing ascent into courtly society brought with it a lawsuit, and to fight the lawsuit Beaumarchais launched into a series of public Memoirs, which cemented his reputation as brilliant, even if he finally landed in jail.

Shortly after, and perhaps in exchange for his release from jail, he set off on his first mission as a secret agent for the king. There was as much gallantry as cloak-and-dagger in his early career: He arranged to block the publication of a pamphlet that besmirched the reputation of Madame du Barry. He had the entire print run burned.

Louis XVI, the new king, sent him to Holland to quash a libelous pamphlet against Queen Marie-Antoinette. He succeeded, but only after a thrilling pursuit through the forests of Germany, a battle with brigands, and arrest and detention as a spy in Vienna.

The best known episode of his life as a spy was his advocacy and then actual management of the supply of war materiel to the American revolutionaries, run through a front company.

HARRIET TUBMAN
UNION SPY AND CONDUCTOR ▶

Harriet Tubman, hailed by abolitionist John Brown as "General" Tubman, worked as a Union spy and the most successful "conductor" on the Underground Railroad, making some 20 increasingly dangerous forays south to lead more than 300 slaves—including her own parents and other family members—to freedom in the North.

She devised clever pieces of tradecraft to safeguard her charges from capture. These included stealing the slaveowner's horse and buggy for the first part of the journey; escaping on Saturday nights, making it impossible to place a runaway advertisement in the newspapers until Monday morning; doubling back south when pursued by slave hunters; and carrying a drug to put restive babies to sleep if their wails threatened to give away the party of escaped slaves.

The biggest prize in any party that Harriet Tubman led would have been herself; by the late 1850s, there were 40,000 dollars worth of southern rewards for her capture. One wanted poster stated that she could not read, and she was in fact illiterate. But when she overheard a group of men discussing this detail in the poster, she pulled out a book she carried with her and pretended to be absorbed in reading it.

Although she was saving about a dozen slaves on each trip south, she made it clear to her charges that she would tolerate no second thoughts. She carried a gun, and would say to those who seemed tired or discouraged: "a live runaway could do great harm by going back, but a dead one could tell no secrets." She would also add, "You'll be free or die." Her most successful—and, we may imagine, gratifying—expedition was during the war, when she helped to guide a small fleet of steamboats up the Combahee River in South Carolina, burning plantations and freeing almost a thousand slaves.

"General" Tubman guided thousands of slaves to freedom.

MOE BERG

THE CATCHER WAS A SPY

Moe Berg wasn't much of a major-league player, but he provided crucial information about Nazi progress on the A-bomb.

Moe Berg was one of the brightest players in prewar major-league baseball. Said one teammate: "He can speak seven languages, but he can't hit in any of them." Actually, Berg spoke 11 languages, and he studied linguistics at Princeton and the Sorbonne. But as one writer observed, the brightest man in baseball has strapped on "the tools of ignorance" (slang for the catcher's kit)—Berg was a catcher.

And the catcher, as the title of one biography puts it, was a spy. It is not known for certain exactly when Berg's career in intelligence began, but many accounts date it to 1934, when Berg accompanied to Japan an exhibition All-Star team that included Babe Ruth and Lou Gehrig. It is not clear, in terms of baseball expertise, what a seldom-used catcher with a batting average of under .250 was doing on that team, but at one point Berg visited St. Luke's Hospital in Tokyo, with a bouquet of flowers for the daughter of U.S. Ambassador Joseph Grew; he never delivered the flowers, and instead went to a top-floor window from which he filmed the skyline and harbor with a home-movie camera. Almost ten years later, the film was used in the planning of Gen. Jimmy Doolittle's 1942 bombing raids on the Japanese capital.

In 1943 Berg parachuted into Yugoslavia to evaluate which of the two networks of anti-Nazi resistance fighters the U.S. should back: He directed American efforts to Tito's partisans. He also traveled to Nazi-occupied Norway as part of the Allied effort to locate and sabotage a heavy-water processing plant that could have been used to make a German atomic bomb. Berg's most famous mission was to Switzerland in 1944 to attend a lecture by Nobel laureate Werner Heisenberg, Nazi Germany's greatest physicist. Berg allegedly carried a pistol, and according to some accounts, if he thought Heisenberg's talk indicated substantial Nazi progress on atomic weapons, he had orders to kill the physicist on the spot. Luckily for both of them, Heisenberg was practically despondent about Germany's prospects.

JOSEPHINE BAKER

UNDERCOVER CHANTEUSE

To hide in plain sight is an old tactic. It plays on the enemy's assumption that something spectacularly obvious can be discounted. So when a St. Louis-born black woman—known variously for dancing in nothing but a G-string festooned with bananas, for broad, cross-eyed mugging, or for strolling down Parisian boulevards dressed to the nines with a lithe leopard on a leash—decided to become a secret agent working against the Nazis, it was the beginning of a magnificent bluff.

If anything, the head of France's Deuxième Bureau was worried that Josephine Baker might turn out to be a double agent. Certainly, her statements in favor of Mussolini's invasion of Abyssinia (modern-day Ethiopia) a few years before might have been worrisome. But Baker, who had become a French citizen, persuaded her future spymasters that she was willing to die for her adopted homeland.

Certainly, France had been good to her. She had grown up poor in America, and racism had restricted her artistic ambitions; in France she was still nothing more than a fabulous curiosity, but as one writer put it, exoticism was certainly preferable to racism.

Ironically, Baker's support of Mussolini afforded her a network of contacts inside the Italian Embassy in Paris; she also had friends in the Japanese Embassy, and she was able to obtain extensive information about German troop movements prior to the invasion of France in May 1940. "La Baker" refused to live in Occupied France, and fled to Vichy France, a vassal state of Nazi Germany, and from there to Spain and Lisbon. With her went sheet music covered with intelligence information penned in invisible ink. Pinned to her undergarments were photographs of sensitive military installations. As she put it, "Who would dare search Josephine Baker?"

...aker was awarded the Croix de Guerre and the Medal of the Resistance.

STIRLING HAYDEN
in Paramount Pictures

P-2725

Hayden was awarded a Silver Star and received a citation from Tito.

STERLING HAYDEN

HUNK OF BURNIN' SPY

Think back on the Stanley Kubrick movie *Dr. Strangelove*, in particular to the improbably named character Col. Jack D. Ripper. He was played by an actor named Sterling Hayden, and he projects a dangerous, demented willingness to do anything, as well as a disgust with the boring, everyday world of routine. Let's put it this way: Sterling Hayden didn't have to pretend very hard to play that role.

Hayden, whose nicknames in the movies (at least according to the publicity offices) were, variously, "The Most Beautiful Man in the Movies" and "The Beautiful Blond Viking God," had a profound distaste for the studio system. He told one interviewer: "When I come into town to talk with a director, I say, 'Who did you really want?' I can tell what's true by their reaction to that question. A lot will fluff it and say, 'Well, we wanted you.' I know damn well they didn't want me. They wanted the biggest name they could find, whether it was Anthony Quinn or John Wayne."

Hayden wasn't a megastar, but he was probably one of the most interesting actors in Hollywood. And the part of his life that he remembered with the greatest love and passion were his years in the OSS.

William Donovan may have recruited him through director John Huston, who was also in the OSS. But unlike Huston and most other big names who wound up in the OSS, Hayden transferred over from the Marine Corps, where he was a captain.

The most exciting portion of his OSS service was certainly his time in Yugoslavia. He regularly ran weapons and other supplies in for Marshal Tito's anti-Nazi guerrilla forces, and smuggled downed Allied airmen back out, via southern Italy. He also helped Tito's partisans blow up railroads and bridges.

LITERARY SPIES

lthough Erskine Childers, whose life and work is described in this chapter, is widely considered the father of the modern spy novel, the early American author James Fenimore Cooper pioneered the genre with his novel *The Spy: A Tale of the Neutral Ground*. As one critic noted, the subtitle is significant: Cooper explores "the ambiguity of a neutral ground wherein secret men do secret things." And it is in literature that we find an ongoing exploration of the semi-pariah status of spies, not unlike theater people in the previous century, both idolized and considered not quite presentable. This chapter tells the stories both of writers who became spies and spies who became writers.

There is a notoriously paradoxical observation about painters and bankers. When they get together, it wryly states, bankers talk about art, and painters talk about money. While it cannot be said with any certainty what spies discuss at their stealthy gatherings, we do know that one of the last achievements of Alan Dulles's long life was to edit a book entitled *Great Spy Stories*.

Playwright Christopher Marlowe's spymaster was Walsingham.

MURDERED CHRISTOPHER MARLOWE

IN SERVICE to the QUEEN

Christopher Marlowe, one of the greatest poets writing in the English language, was in touch with his dark side, as we might put it nowadays. His plays dealt with sinister if powerful figures: Tamerlane, the barbarian shepherd who rose to immense power through his ambition and brutality; Dr. Faustus, an overweening scholar who sold his immortal soul to the devil in exchange for worldly wealth and pleasure; Edward II, the weak, homosexual king of England who was overthrown, imprisoned, and executed by his wife and son; and Barabas, the "Jew of Malta," an unscrupulous businessman whose story is preceded by a speech placed in the mouth of Niccolò Machiavelli, an Italian political author considered so diabolical in England at the time that his name became slang for Lucifer himself: Old Nick.

Marlowe's problem, people might say with a knowing nod, started in college. In fact, he was pretty certainly recruited while at Cambridge to work in Sir Francis Walsingham's espionage service. It is believed he was sent to Rheims in France to infiltrate a Catholic plot against the queen (this at a time when the two world superpowers were Catholic and Protestant, and the term "popish," used in England, sounded roughly like Commie in the American fifties). His prolonged absences, and fear that he was actually planning to defect to the Catholic side and betray Protestant England, led the university to refuse to issue him a degree. A letter from the Queen's Privy Council, stating that Marlowe had been engaged "on matters touching the benefit of his country," released the degree.

His grisly murder in 1593, three years after the death of his spymaster, Walsingham, may have been in the line of duty, or it may simply have come when Walsingham could no longer protect him.

~~DANIEL~~ DANIEL DEFOE

NON-CONFORMIST SPY

The first thing anyone learns about Daniel Defoe is a lie: his name. Names were slippery things in those days: In three letters written to the same person in the same year, Defoe signed himself variously D. Foe, de Foe, and Daniel Defoe. But he was born Daniel Foe.

He is said to have been quite adept at assuming names. His path into—and out of—espionage was an erratic one and involved his feigning of religious and political beliefs.

He came into the world a "non-conformist," which in those days meant "not church of England." He received an excellent, though non-conformist, education, and launched into business at an early age. In his early 20s, Defoe joined the Duke of Monmouth's great—and unsuccessful—rebellion against the new king, James II. By his mid-30s, he had experienced a crushing bankruptcy, but had also become a personal acquaintance of the "glorious and immortal" (his own fawning words) King William III. Influential court friendships won him profitable office and allowed him to write freely. It was the writing that led to his downfall, and to espionage.

After William died and Anne succeeded to the throne, Defoe wrote an anonymous satirical religious tract entitled *The Shortest Way with Dissenters*, calling for savage treatment of non-Anglicans. Many high churchmen gleefully endorsed the tract and were enraged when it was revealed as satire.

A warrant was issued for Defoe (the charge was seditious libel), and the only personal description we have of him accompanied the 1703 wanted bulletin: "a middle-size spare man, about 40 years old, of a brown complexion, and dark-brown coloured hair, but wears a wig, a hooked nose, a sharp chin, grey eyes, and a large mole near his mouth."

Defoe is quoted as having said, "Intelligence is the soul of all public business."

Defoe threw himself on the court's mercy, but was sentenced to a fine and three stands in the pillory. Defoe wittily turned the punishment into a triumph. He wrote the daring "Hymn To The Pillory," and as he stood in the stocks, the poem was being hawked in the streets, the mob applauded him, and the pillory itself was garlanded with flowers.

He was finally released from prison through the intercession of Queen Anne's favorite, Robert Harley, secretary of state. Before long, he was embarking on secret missions on the government's behalf, and had in fact been released on condition that he become a secret agent.

Defoe's espionage activity took many forms. He traveled the British Isles under cover, using the "legend" of Alexander Goldsmith, a trades-man, submitting reports on his observations. He went to Scotland several times while the problematic unification with England was under way. One of his subtlest areas of work was as an editor for the Jacobite publication Mist's Journal, on the agreement with the government that he would tone down the political opinions published therein.

BENJAMIN FRANKLIN
COLONIAL CORRESPONDENT

Benjamin Franklin was one of the most famous men of his day. As a scientist, inventor, author, publisher, statesman, and diplomat, he was fêted throughout his time in Paris as ambassador for the United States; images of him were everywhere, from snuffboxes to chamber pots, wearing his fur hat and wire-rim eyeglasses, weirdly foreshadowing hippie garb two centuries later. He was the center of a social feeding frenzy, and he clearly understood that there was no better place to hide than in plain sight.

Franklin, as one of the three members of the Committee of Secret Correspondence—established by the Continental Congress as a sort of early intelligence clearinghouse—ran an array of operations. Some involved propaganda and disinformation: Franklin devised the idea of disguising as tobacco packets an offer of land grants to Hessian mercenaries defecting from British service, thus targeting ordinary soldiers, an innovative use of printer's technology. Another piece of propaganda was a letter he forged, purportedly from a German prince, urging his officers to let wounded soldiers die; as surviving cripples they were unfit for service.

One of his most spectacular acts of espionage, technically a piece of covert action, took place in England in late 1776 and early 1777. In a sense Franklin was the first American "chief of station" abroad, and a highly successful one. The operation involved a young man known as John the Painter. Just as Allied intelligence later identified German ball-bearing factories as strategic bombing targets, John the Painter explained that destroying all the British navy's rope could paralyze its war effort. He was given an enthusiastic go-ahead, and before year's end, he had set the dockyards at Portsmouth ablaze.

Franklin used his extensive literary skills to undermine the British.

Childers may have hastened the beginning of World War I with his no

ERSKINE CHILDERS

FATHER OF THE SPY NOVEL

Irish-born Erskine Childers was a cousin of a first lord of the admiralty, who was also secretary for war. That family influence, plus his own fascination with yachting along the German coast, especially the intricate tidal waterways along the Frisian islands, led to his only novel, The Riddle of the Sands (1903). (The family influence continued: Childers's son was president of Ireland.)

The book was a spy novel; it was popular and influential. So influential, in fact, that the first edition included a clarifying postscript from the charismatic First Sea Lord, Jackie Fisher (more formally known as Adm. Sir John Arbuthnot Fisher, First Baron Fisher).

The note read: "It so happens that while this book was in the press a number of measures have been taken by the Government to counteract some of the very weaknesses and dangers which are alluded to above. A Committee of National Defence has been set up, and the welcome given to it was a truly extraordinary comment on the apathy and confusion which it is designed to supplant. A site on the Forth has been selected for a new North Sea naval base—an excellent if tardy decision; for ten years or so must elapse before the existing anchorage becomes in any sense a 'base.' A North Sea fleet has also been created—another good measure; but it should be remembered that its ships are not modern, or in the least capable of meeting the principal German squadrons under the circumstances supposed above."

What was all the fuss about? In Childers's account, a snobbish, effete clerk in the British Foreign Ministry is at loose ends as to how to spend his summer holidays. Unexpectedly, a telegram arrives from the Frisian coast, and the young snob's interest is piqued. Before long, he finds himself aboard a decidedly down-market sailboat, threading his way through the dangerous tidal rips and sandflats of the north German coast.

Spy stories were different then (Great Britain did not even officially recognize the possibility of there being such a thing as a spy in peacetime until 1911), and what might today involve a great deal of intent typing and Net-browsing and cell phoning, a hundred years ago involved relentless sounding and chart-reading and close-hauling. Navigation was to the British Empire at the turn of the last century what web-surfing is to the American empire at the turn of this one.

If you are planning to read *The Riddle of the Sands*, then by all means stop here. If you are not, there are three strands being woven together here.

The first is the gradual realization in Carruthers, the narrator, of just how idle and frivolous his upper-class concerns really are. The book opens with this remarkably languid phrase, which might well have been uttered by a young man stretched out on a chaise longue: "I [am] a young man of condition and fashion, who knows the right people, belongs to the right clubs, has a safe, possibly a brilliant, future in the Foreign Office—[and such a man] may be excused for a sense of complacent martyrdom, when, with his keen appreciation of the social calendar, he is doomed to the outer solitude of London in September."

The second is a growing appreciation for the skill and determination of his newfound (and decidedly lower-class) yachting partner, Davies. "[He was not] one of my immediate set; but we were a sociable college, and I had seen a good deal of him, liking him for his physical energy combined with a certain simplicity and modesty."

The third strand is the emerging German plan for an invasion of England with a flotilla of flat-bottomed barges that will be launched from the sleepy seaside Frisian villages fronting the tidal sandflats on the northern coast.

It is difficult to appreciate the startling effect of this idea on the British public in the early years of the century. It had long been thought in England that if there was going to be a war with any nation, it would most likely be with France (after all, the imperial houses of Russia and Germany contained blood relations of the recently deceased Empress Victoria). The immediate, indirect result of the publication of The Riddle of the Sands was the acceleration of Britain's program for the construction of big-gun, heavily armed warships, known as dreadnoughts. Germany responded in kind, and the naval arms race surely contributed to the outbreak of World War I.

It has been observed that the most popular hobbies were once critically important means of livelihood: gardening, hunting, woodworking, and of course sailing. If so, Childers was portraying his own favorite hobby as something of crucial importance to the nation. Ironically, if his book contributed to World War I, there could not have been a more dangerous way of glorifying a hobby.

Yachting had other dangerous applications in Childers's life. He became a supporter of Irish home rule years after he wrote his book, and some reports state that guns that he brought to Ireland in his yacht in 1914 were used in the Easter uprising of 1916.

He became increasingly involved in Irish politics, and in 1922 was arrested for possession of a small revolver that had been a gift from IRA commander Michael Collins. Though there was no evidence that he had ever used the gun, he was found guilty and sentenced to execution by firing squad.

GRAHAM GREENE

THE QUIET BRIT

In 1949 a British magazine called the New Statesman held a Graham Greene parody contest. The second-place winner, writing under a pseudonym, was actually none other than Graham Greene, the famous novelist himself.

Wit, deviousness, and irony are all part of the Graham Greene legend. They were also present to some extent in his intelligence work, or at least in his published opinions about that work.

One element of his time in MI6—during World War II he was an operative in Sierra Leone and in Portugal—that he discussed was his case officer, none other than Harold "Kim" Philby, the notorious Soviet spy.

"No one could have been a better chief," Greene wrote about him. "He had all the small loyalties to his colleagues, and of course his big loyalty was unknown to us."

And yet Greene remained close to Philby even after the former British agent escaped to Moscow.

Greene sent a copy of the manuscript for The Human Factor to Philby in Moscow to ask him his opinion. It later emerged that elements of the story—about a secret treaty between Great Britain and South Africa to keep South African gold out of Soviet hands—were actually reflected in an existing secret treaty.

Perhaps Graham Greene's writing about Vietnam is what comes most vividly to mind when his intelligence links are mentioned. Specifically, the figure of Howard Pyle—a naïve American king-maker whose bumbling leads to war—is said to be based on Col. Edward Lansdale, an American intelligence officer whom Greene met while working as a journalist in Indochina.

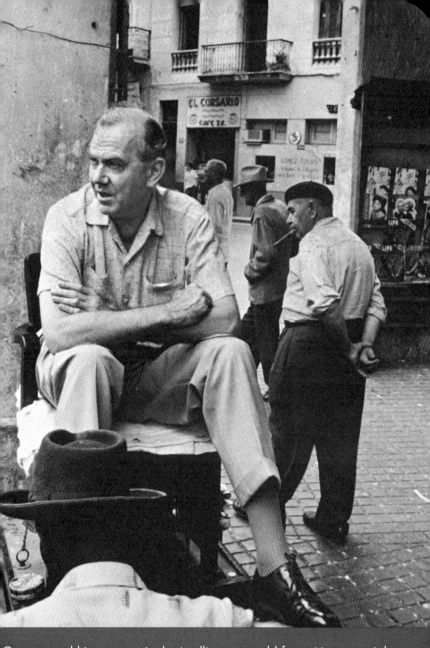
Greene used his contacts in the intelligence world for writing material.

Fleming invented Bond-like scenarios for British naval intelligence.

IAN FLEMING

BOND, JAMES BOND

The life of Ian Fleming, the creator of Commander James Bond, is a remarkable story, and all the more remarkable for being so different from that of Agent 007. The Bond stories are pure art, a mixture of a highly imaginative and reasonably authentic portrayal of intelligence gathering and covert action. But Fleming's life is the frame within which that painting is set, the structure that made it possible.

To begin with, he descended from remarkable stock. His grandfather, Robert Fleming, was a poor Scotsman from the town of Dundee who entered into finance in the late 19th century. He pioneered Scottish investment funds in the booming, post-Civil War American economy, and before long he had founded his own bank (his family recently sold the bank to Chase, for a price said to be around three billion dollars).

Ian Fleming's father, Valentine Fleming, was killed in World War I, but his will left his entire estate of a quarter million pounds to Ian's mother; when his grandfather died, that estate went to Ian's uncle. So by the time Ian was 25, he had been cut out of two wills; his mother had the right to cut him out of her will if she so chose.

His mother, an imperious, powerful woman, kept her hold over Fleming for the rest of his life. In fact, he died less than three weeks after she did, and made only a relative pittance from the entire Bond franchise (about 100,000 pounds). His nickname for her was "Emmie," and it has been ventured that the irascible, powerful spymaster "M" in the Bond novels was actually modeled on Fleming's mother.

His educational history was spotty, at best. He—like Commander Bond—left Eton under a cloud; he chose to leave the military academy of Sandhurst after one year. He completed his education at a private academy in the Tyrolean Alps—under the very un-Bond-like tutorship of disciples of the psychiatrist Alfred Adler.

Apparently, Fleming had a crushing inferiority complex that needed to be overcome. But the Alps were also a playground and a theater for his imagination. One friend from that period remembers driving up a steep hill behind a truck carrying heavy machinery. Fleming explained that if they were chasing the truck, all that would be needed to stop them was to cut the ropes, and the heavy machinery would crash down on their car, smashing them to smithereens—a trick that appears in *Moonraker*.

After his difficulties in school, Fleming experienced another failure—he was passed over at the Foreign Service examination. But he managed to land a job as an editor at the news agency Reuters, and in 1933 he was sent to Moscow to cover the trial of six British engineers arrested for sabotage. Many of his Russian villains must have come out of this grim, Stalinesque experience; in fact, Fleming wrote a note to Stalin requesting an interview and received a handwritten note from the great dictator rejecting his request. His coverage was very popular back in England, and he was next offered a trip to Germany to interview Hitler. But Fleming chose to become a stockbroker.

And oddly enough, that choice led directly to the intelligence service. His family ties—his grandfather's bank, his father's heroic death in World War I—and a little intelligence work that he had done in Russia in the late thirties meant that when the director of naval intelligence, Rear Adm. John Godfrey, needed a personal assistant, the choice fell on Ian Fleming.

The admiralty office in which Fleming worked, Room 39, was described as resembling an Arab bank in Tangier or Beirut: "the same tightly packed desks and never-diminishing piles of paper, the same din of telephones and typewriters." But to Ian Fleming it was heaven.

Here, he came up with ideas for operations of all sorts.

Blowing up the dam across the Iron Gates of the Danube, parachuting into Berlin to assassinate Hitler, sinking giant blocks of cement into the Channel, with men with periscopes and radios inside—"a lot of Ian's ideas were just plain crazy...but a lot of his far-fetched ideas had just that glimmer of possibility in them that made you think twice before you threw them in the wastepaper basket," recalled an admiral who worked with him.

Glamour and danger seemed to seep in equal parts into the enterprises that Fleming undertook. At one point Admiral Darlan, chief of the French navy, had left Paris during the collapse of France in the summer of 1940. The British had been negotiating with Darlan for the handover of the French navy, fourth largest on Earth, with plenty of modern, powerful ships. Fleming was sent to France with a radioman, and he served as a tenuous link in the negotiations—the setting was a château built by Coty, the cosmetics king, a panoply of magnificence until Stuka dive bombers attacked the place.

Immediately thereafter, Fleming headed for Bordeaux, where he oversaw the evacuation of many well-to-do British civilians, until amid the Bentleys and Rolls-Royces "a cavalcade of enormous motorcars appeared...carrying King Zog of Albania, his family, and mountains of luggage, including the crown jewels of Albania."

Fleming flew to New York with Admiral Godfrey for secret meetings with J. Edgar Hoover, William Stevenson, and William Donovan. When they deplaned, there was a crowd of newspaper photographers popping their flashes at their fellow passenger fashion designer Elsa Schiapparelli. In the background of the photographs that appeared in the next day's newspapers were a startled and disconcerted director of British Naval Intelligence and his personal assistant, the creator of James Bond. And the rest, of course, is spy fiction.

British intelligence officials hated the spy world that le Carré created

JOHN LE CARRÉ

CREATOR OF THE ANTI-BOND

Like James Angleton and Kim Philby (or for that matter, William F. Buckley), John le Carré had a father who was larger than life and twice as complicated.

As Frank Conroy wrote in a review of a le Carré novel, "*A Perfect Spy* contains autobiographical elements. Mr. le Carré's mother vanished when he was quite young, his father was a confidence man who once spent some time in jail, and at another time ran for Parliament. (An exact parallel with Rick Pym in the book.) Magnus Pym's experiences, traveling as a student, being recruited into British intelligence, etc., seem to fit what we know, or can guess, about young le Carré." Le Carré himself later wrote, "So we found ourselves, my brother and I, living in the style of millionaire paupers."

And to make the trio even more intertwined, John le Carré's cover was actually blown by Philby while le Carré was still just David Cornwell, a deskbound intelligence officer attached to the British Embassy in Germany. Deskbound he may have been, but at a certain point he was given the post of British consul in Hamburg (one has to wonder if Graham Greene had le Carré in mind when he chose the title of his novel *The Honorary Consul*; Greene claims that the title came to him in a dream).

Le Carré had made his way into intelligence through an unlikely path: As a freelance illustrator, he did the drawings for *Talking Birds*, a book written by the one-time head of MI5, Maxwell Knight, also a sometime naturalist.

John le Carré began writing spy novels at a time when Ian Fleming was especially popular. And le Carré was certainly the anti-Ian Fleming, just as his characters were arguably anti-James Bonds.

He claims to have coined his pseudonym from a phrase spotted by chance in a shop window. Perhaps he unconsciously had the name of Mathilde Carré in mind, a French triple agent who was in equal measures hapless and cunning.

In any case, the world he created, as Frank Conroy noted, owed as much to Charles Dickens as it did to any of the other masters of spy literature: "He has skipped over John Buchan, W. Somerset Maugham, Wilkie Collins et al. and gone to the master, who died writing The Mystery of Edwin Drood. (A sad piece of work that would doubtless have been even sadder had it been finished.)"

Sad is a term that nicely describes the world that le Carré has created. There is never an overarching ideal, a sense of impending victory. There is little moral distinction between the two sides in a Game that no longer seems Great. The characters are driven by obsession, a resigned sense of duty, fatalism—if Dickens is present, Graham Greene is there too.

One critic noted that le Carré's "famous hero is George Smiley, a Chekhovian character and shadowlike member of the British Foreign Service." Le Carré himself described Smiley, through the unreliable, though reliably unpleasant, character of Smiley's ex-wife Ann, as "breathtakingly ordinary," and "Short, fat, and of a quiet disposition, he appeared to spend a lot of money on really bad clothes, which hung about his squat frame like a skin on a shrunken toad." The reference to Chekhov and the wraithlike and yet shabby quality suggests le Carré's basic theme of the damage that the secret world could do to a normal human psyche. Certainly, the locus of le Carré's fascination with secrets, as he has admitted himself, was his toxic and dishonest relationship with his father.

Interestingly, his brother, Rupert Cornwell, is a respected financial journalist perhaps best known for his coverage of and book about

Roberto Calvi, as close to an international black-bag trickmaster as the financial arena offers. Calvi wound up hanged—despite an initial British government finding to the contrary, he was clearly murdered—beneath the Blackfriars Bridge in London, possibly an obscure hint at the secret Masonic lodge in which Calvi was involved. If there is a real-world counterpart to le Carré's dispiriting world of ruthless machinations, it would have to be in the shadow land of Italian (and Vatican: Calvi was known as God's Banker, the title of Rupert Cornwell's book) finance and intelligence services.

And yet there is a set of literary forebears to le Carré's characters not generally invoked: Both Dashiell Hammett and Raymond Chandler offered characters who were unromantic in their encounters with crime and double-dealing. One of Hammett's main characters, the Continental Op, was in fact a short, fat detective. Chandler's characters, from John Dalmas to Philip Marlowe, live behind "a reasonably shabby door at the end of a reasonably shabby corridor in the sort of building that was new about the year the all-tile bathroom became the basis of civilization."

Wisecracks aside, the sensibility is quite similar.

And that sensibility ruffled quite a few feathers in the intelligence world. To quote from the authoritative *Spy Book*, "Most intelligence officials in Britain hated the spy world that le Carré portrayed. In *Literary Agents* (1987), Anthony Masters quotes from an unpublished manuscript by John Bingham, who was both an intelligence officer and a writer. Clearly targeting le Carré, Bingham wrote, 'The belief encouraged by many spy writers that Intelligence officers consisted of moles, morons, shits and homosexuals makes the Intelligence job no easier.'"

But le Carré did not limit his acid view of the world to espionage. His novels have also discussed the worlds of terrorism and pharmaceutical multinationals.

AGENTS OF
INFLUENCE

SPIES WHO PULLED STRINGS

Of all the vague and elusive areas of espionage, the work of agents of influence--used to exert covert influence on another nation's leaders, media, or pressure groups--is surely the foggiest. The KGB had an agent of influence in almost every Western capital, the Nazis had their agents of influence in the Western democracies, and there has been a recent increase in the number of incidents involving agents of influence for the People's Republic of China.

One of the reasons for the vagueness of the status of agents of influence is that by simply registering as a lobbyist or publicist for a foreign power, agents of influence could pursue their endeavors legally. But the moment an agent of influence became known as a paid-- or simply official--advocate for a foreign power, his or her influence would also plummet.

One of the more surprising agents of influence in this chapter is Sir William Wiseman, who wormed his way into the good graces of Colonel House, President Woodrow Wilson's right-hand man. House had no official position, but enormous say over the running of the government. And Wiseman helped to sway House, and Wilson, in their decision to enter WWI.

WILLIAM WISEMAN

BRINGING the U.S. into WORLD WAR I

Sir William Wiseman had to knock around a bit before he found his calling. At Cambridge he had been a champion college boxer, but that didn't fit with the inherited title of baronet and a long family tradition of service in the British navy. He tried his hand at journalism, but couldn't get published; he wrote plays, but they weren't produced.

Then came the First World War. After surviving a gas attack in Flanders, he joined Britain's foreign intelligence service and was sent to the United States. Later that year, President Woodrow Wilson was re-elected with the slogan "He Kept Us Out of War." It became Wiseman's job to help bring the U.S. into the war.

In 1917 Wiseman obtained $75,000 from the Wilson Administration to send an agent to revolutionary Russia, in an attempt to keep the Russians in the war and the Bolsheviks out of power. The agent they sent was Somerset Maugham, history records with what success.

Wiseman did better as an agent of influence himself; the key to his success was Col. Edward House, Wilson's trusted confidant and adviser. House had been instrumental in the election of Texas Governor James Hogg (who so famously named his daughter Ima), and rose to power after helping Wilson secure the Democratic nomination for the 1912 presidential elections.

Edward House was tremendously impressed by the "efficient" Wiseman. And the youthful Wiseman superbly exploited House's fatherly feelings; House was childless and lonely. It was later noted, in a book that Sigmund Freud co-wrote, that House "habitually permitted Sir William Wiseman, head of the British Secret Service in the United States, to sit in his private office in New York and read the most secret documents of the American government."

Wiseman, center, used his upper-class charm to influence U.S. policy.

HARRY DEXTER WHITE

NEW DEAL FOR THE KREMLIN ▶

The conspiracy-theorist, "black-helicopter" crowd can point to Harry Dexter White with righteous indignation. He did not become a Soviet agent until after he completed extensive academic studies (when he was almost 40) at Columbia, Stanford, and Harvard. He then went on to play a major role in the founding of the International Monetary Fund and the World Bank and helped to brief the Soviet delegation to the 1945 conference that established the UN, giving the Soviets inside knowledge of the U.S. negotiating position.

How influential was he? Well, in 2002 Kenneth Rogoff, director of research at the IMF, wrote, "Sometimes I spend my nights re-reading how Englishman John Maynard Keynes and American Harry Dexter White calmly traded ideas for reshaping the international financial system, even as the second world war exploded around them." Well, as they did so, White may have been putting in a word for his pals in the Kremlin.

Henry Wallace, FDR's third-term Vice President, said that had he succeeded to the Presidency, he planned to appoint Harry Dexter White secretary of the Treasury. White—with Keynes—was the dominating figure at the Bretton Woods Conference and the chief economist at the Yalta Conference in 1944.

At Yalta, it is thought that White's advice encouraged FDR to accept a reparations figure for the U.S.S.R. of ten billion dollars more than the British were willing to accept. And at another point that year, apparently, White provided the Soviets with samples of planned U.S. currency for occupied Germany. The Soviets then demanded plates, ink, and paper samples, and when the Bureau of Engraving objected, White insisted, somewhat indignantly. The Russians then printed

White promoted Soviet interests while serving FDR.

currency of their own, identical in every way to the American currency.

Historians and authors still disagree, vociferously at times, about the extent of White's espionage, and hence, treason. He died of a heart attack before a trial could determine his innocence or guilt. But there seems to be general agreement that he was, at the very least, an agent of influence, meaning that he used his positions of considerable power and prestige to further Soviet interests.

Prosecutors feared that Leung had tainted U.S. intelligence.

KATRINA LEUNG

A CHINESE AFFAIR

In late December 2005, Katrina Leung made a plea bargain to a few minor charges that will allow her to face probation and a cash fine for lying about a sexual affair and filing a false tax return. Part of the income that she failed to report was $35,000 in payments from the FBI. But she will not face prison time, a dismaying end to a case that prosecutors hoped would show that two decades of U.S. intelligence about China had been tainted by disinformation planted by a highly placed double agent.

Katrina Leung was born Man Ying Chan, in Guangzhou province, China, to a family that was well connected with the Chinese ruling hierarchy. And those family ties made her especially valuable to the FBI, which paid her almost two million dollars for the intelligence she provided. But it emerged in recent years that she had been having an affair with her FBI handler, a counterintelligence specialist. Both she and the handler were married.

She has also been accused of being a Chinese double agent.

Leung is thought to have had an affair with another FBI agent, and the ramifications of her complex operations may have affected such cases as the TRW espionage case described in the book and film *The Falcon and the Snowman*, the Wen Ho Lee case, and various cases involving China and American campaign finance violations.

As the *Washington Monthly* put it: "Democrats...can take a measure of satisfaction from this unlikely coda: The only bonafide Chinese spy so far turns out to have been not only a Republican, but a well-connected GOP fundraiser. And not just any Republican fundraiser, but one who happened to be sleeping with one of the lead FBI agents investigating Democratic fundraising."

COVERT ACTORS
AND WETWORKERS

WALKING THE WALK

wide variety of activities can be described under the heading "covert action." Covert action can extend to such subtle ploys as disinformation. (The Russians have excelled in disinformation, but the Americans have done their share: Arnaud de Borchgrave, editor of the *Washington Times* and a former *Newsweek* correspondent, says that when America does it, it is not disinformation, it "is management of the news.") Whatever the name, it is certainly one of the tamest forms of covert action. Gen. Sir Frank Kitson invented a form of counterinsurgency action involving "pseudo-gangs," which infiltrated and helped to defeat the Mau Maus in Kenya. Soviet agent Ramon Mercader was a wetworker (spy lingo for assassin) who killed one of Stalin's ideological rivals, Leon Trotsky. Maj. Gen. Edward Lansdale was involved in planning for a potential assassination attempt on Cuba's leader (or dictator), Fidel Castro; among the methods considered was a box of exploding cigars.

A cottage publishing industry has grown up to document covert action around the world. One of the classic vehicles for journalism on the subject is the energetic left-wing publication *Covert Action Quarterly*.

EDWARD LANSDALE
THE QUIET AMERICAN

It has become almost commonplace to identify the title character of Graham Greene's novel *The Quiet American* as a fictionalized portrait of Maj. Gen. Edward Lansdale, an unorthodox clandestine operative who worked in the Philippines, Vietnam, and in the American intelligence establishment, where he was viewed with some distrust as a maverick.

But Graham Greene denied this portrayal, saying he would never have used Lansdale "to represent the danger of innocence."

Greene's career really began when the Second World War ended. Before the war he had drifted into the exciting new world of advertising, but after Pearl Harbor he volunteered for the army. He failed to pass the physical examination; he appealed and was accepted for "limited" duty. He worked for the OSS, writing manuals and developing intelligence.

After the war, he was sent to the Philippines, where he first encountered the Huk insurgency. Later, working for the Office of Policy Coordination—a secret organization for covert action, which operated outside of the CIA—he helped to engineer the election of President Ramón Magsaysay. Among other unorthodox techniques he employed, he spread rumors that a local vampire was hunting down the Huks (he would then have anti-Huk guerrillas kill a few Huks by draining them of blood through puncture wounds in the neck), or he would publicly thank Huks in order to sow dissension in their ranks.

He also worked on Project Mongoose, the campaign to eliminate Cuban dictator Fidel Castro, through assassination if necessary (memorably, the idea of poisoning his cigars was floated).

Exploding cigars and vampire scares were two of Lansdale's most outrageous proposals for covert action.

But his biggest operation was in Vietnam. He was a houseguest and adviser to South Vietnamese President Ngo Dinh Diem; but his presence in Vietnam was unwelcome both to the outgoing French administration and to the local CIA chief of station, who saw him as an unpredictable rival. One of his operations was a psychological ploy: persuading nearly a million Vietnamese Catholics to flee the north, resulting in a refugee crisis and dismaying world news reports.

RAMÓN MERCADER
STONE-COLD ICEPICK KILLER

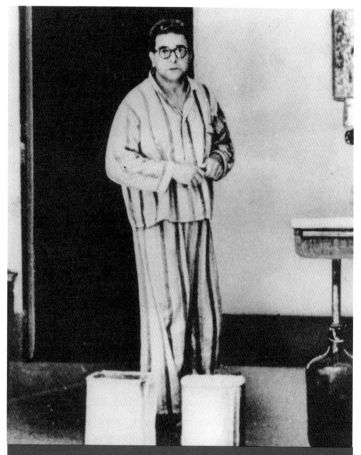

Mercader was said to have "unusually rapid reaction time," and "an almost photographic memory," among other skills.

Interestingly, Stalin thought he could probably strike a deal with Hitler, but was obsessed with the need to eliminate Leon Trotsky, Lenin's lieutenant and would-be successor. With the benefit of hindsight, you might say he had his priorities reversed. But then again, Trotsky was vulnerable, and Hitler was quite well protected.

By the time Trotsky fetched up in Mexico, he had been an exile from the center of Soviet power for almost ten years, since his losing battle to replace Lenin. He lived in a fortified villa in Coyoacán, on the outskirts of Mexico City, guarded by the few remaining Trotskyites, members of competing factions but united in their reverence for Trotsky.

By the late thirties Trotsky was being tried in absentia for treason as the chief co-conspirator in the first great Soviet show trial; his image was already beginning to be cropped and airbrushed out of official photographs of the pioneers of Russian Communism. But that was not enough.

Stalin personally ordered the head of the NKVD's Administration for Special Tasks (his career on the upswing after a successful assassination of an undesirable "counterrevolutionary" with a booby-trapped assortment pack of bonbons) to kill Trotsky, an operation that was code-named "Duck."

The first attempt on Trotsky's life came in late May 1940. It was led in part by the Mexican muralist David Siqueiros; 20 men stormed the villa (admitted by a naïve American guard, who was kidnapped and killed), machine guns and revolvers blazing. Incredibly, Trotsky, his wife, and his grandson all survived the attack by hiding under beds; a Molotov cocktail was thrown into the five-year-old's room, where the boy cowered under his bed.

This is where the Spanish-born Ramón Mercader came into play. He was the most important member (code name Raymond) of the illegal network run by his Stalinist mother, Caridad Mercader del Río. He had received training in assassinations in Moscow and may have been involved in the killing of the German Rudolf Klement, who had been in charge of organizing the Fourth International Congress (an anti-Stalin revolutionary organization) in the fall of 1938. Certainly, Ramón Mercader was present at the conference; Klement was not. His headless body had washed up along the banks of the Seine, only to be identified by distinctive scars on the hands.

A few months earlier, Trotsky's son Lev Sedov had died mysteriously following an operation for appendicitis; historians generally agree that he was murdered.

Now only the great apostate, Trotsky himself, remained at large. The military-style assault had failed miserably. Something more subtle was called for.

Ramón Mercader was in position. He had begun a relationship with an American Trotskyite, Sylvia Ageloff, who later became Trotsky's secretary in Mexico City. Mercader was cautious and patient. He would drive Sylvia to work each morning and pick her up each evening, smiling at the guards and never attempting to enter the villa.

But once the attack failed in late May 1940, he began to implement his penetration of the villa. He first met Trotsky just a few days later. At one point, when Mercader traveled to New York, he loaned Trotsky his Buick. He made a present of a toy glider to Trotsky's grandson and taught him how to fly it. He was endlessly agreeable and only made ten or so visits over three months.

Much has been made of Mercader as a killer. He was intelligent, fluent in several languages, and an athlete. One account reports that he had "unusually rapid reaction time, an almost photographic memory, the ability to find his way in the dark, the capacity to learn quickly and remember complex instructions." Certainly, he fooled the reportedly unattractive Sylvia Ageloff into believing he was in love with her, and he succeeded in working his way into the Trotsky entourage.

On August 21 1940, as the Battle of Britain was raging and the Soviet Union was contentedly digesting Estonia, Lithuania, and Latvia, Ramón Mercader brought a magazine article he had written to Trotsky for his approval and comments.

In one pocket of his raincoat was a short-handled Alpine climbing axe, or pick, often described as an icepick, with one blunt end and one sharp end. According to Mercader's account, as Trotsky sat at his desk reading the article, Mercader gripped the axe with both hands, closed his eyes, and slammed the axe into Trotsky's skull. According to one account, he used the broad end of the axe instead of the sharp end.

Mercader had hoped Trotsky would die silently; instead he let out "a terrible piercing cry" (which the cold-blooded Mercader admitted he would hear "all my life"). Trotsky's bodyguards burst into the room and beat Mercader savagely; reportedly Trotsky was sufficiently alert to tell them to stop the beating.

Trotsky died the next day. The police staged a confrontation between Sylvia Ageloff and Mercader; apparently a distraught Ageloff begged her lover to tell the truth, only to break down completely when he admitted that their relationship had been a ploy to gain access to the villa.

Mercader was tried and sentenced to 20 years in prison, the maximum term in Mexico at the time. After his release he settled in Moscow, where he lived for nearly another 20 years. He was named a Hero of the Soviet Union and given a free apartment and a generous pension. The murder of Trotsky has largely been forgotten. Grotesquely, in 1972 (while Mercader was still alive) Joseph Losey made a movie about it, with Richard Burton as Trotsky and Alain Delon as Ramón Mercader.

FRANK KITSON

COUNTERINSURGENT SPECIALIST

NO PHOTO
ON FILE

Kitson is perhaps best known for his role in "Bloody Sunday."

Gen. Sir Frank Kitson of the British army was for many years a highly regarded theorist—and practitioner—of counterinsurgency tactics, which he summarized in two books: Low Intensity Operations and Gangs and Counter-Gangs.

He served in Kenya, Cyprus, and Malaya, all the settings for insurgencies that the British worked to suppress. Perhaps more disturbing, he also served in Belfast, Northern Ireland, in the early 1970s and was recently a witness in the British government hearings into the army shootings of civilians in 1972 remembered as "Bloody Sunday."

His theory of "pseudo-gangs" was first implemented in Kenya, during the uprising of the anti-British, nationalist Mau Mau guerrillas, some 20,000 of whom had taken to the forest. He is thought to have originated the term "low intensity operations."

His approach to the situation in Kenya was to organize countergangs, or pseudo-gangs, of friendly Kikuyu tribesmen, who infiltrated the Mau Mau guerrilla forces (also Kikuyus) by pretending to be terrorists themselves. The insurgency was successfully undermined.

Kitson's approach was recently praised in an article by a professor at the Naval Postgraduate Institute in Monterey, California, as one that the Bush Administration could learn from.

Other comments have been less admiring. One author wrote, "His counterinsurgency program rippled even further, touching nearly every corner of the world where Britain had imperial and strategic interests.... In Kenya they broke civilian support by systematizing torture, inflicting heavy civilian casualties, and detaining nearly 1.5 million Africans thought to be sympathetic to the Mau Mau."

According to that author, Kitson's real legacy was an extensive body of emergency legislation in countries formerly British.

Kitson is still alive as of this writing, and his most recent book, interestingly, was a biography of Oliver Cromwell, a figure whose role in British history was every bit as controversial as Kitson's own, a revolutionary commander whose reputation was blotted by his brutality in Ireland.

DOMINIQUE PRIEUR

RAINBOW WARRIOR KILLER

This is less a story of the life of Dominique Prieur than of the life that she helped to take. In covert action, quite often, the victims are tough operators, people as callous and dangerous as their murderers.

But Capt. Dominique Prieur, alias Sophie Turenge, was involved in the 1985 French government-ordered bombing of the *Rainbow Warrior*, a ship owned by Greenpeace and about to set out on a campaign of protests against French atmospheric nuclear testing in the South Pacific.

Prieur later claimed that the French secret agents had done everything they could to ensure that there was no loss of life. In the planning for the attack, the easiest operative approach would have been to bomb the ship while it was at sea, she wrote, but they chose to do the bombing while the ship was docked.

It is not clear what operative advantage there would have been to bombing the ship at sea (instead of at dock), but Prieur's shock at the death caused by the attack rings hollow. Sinking a ship with people on board, and without warning, seems likely to cause loss of life. And considering the sloppy tradecraft—working under their real names, hanging around after the explosion, or in a word, getting caught—the agents may not have been the sharpest tools in the covert shed.

Indeed, as the ship began to sink, a Dutch crew member and photographer named Fernando Pereira went below, perhaps to get his cameras, and was surprised by a second explosion. He drowned as the *Rainbow Warrior* settled to the bottom.

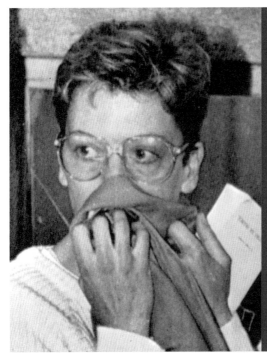

Capt. Dominique Prieur, the French agent spearheading the bombing of the *Rainbow Warrior*, a Greenpeace ship, implausibly maintained that all efforts were made to ensure no loss of life.

As the French agents rushed back to Auckland, the capital of New Zealand, from the port, Prieur made a call to an emergency number: "Hi, how are you? It's Sophie here. I'm calling from New Zealand. The holidays aren't going too well, I've got a big health problem. I'm ill and I really want to come home. What's more, we've been worried about the camper van. Our holidays in camper vans are finished, that's for sure."

Prieur and another French agent were convicted of the killing, but served only two years of their sentence in New Zealand before being repatriated to France.

North was a covert actor implementing orders from higher up the chai

OLIVER NORTH

COVERT SHREDDER, ABOVE THE LAW

Few spies are as well known as Oliver North has been for the past 20 years. He has written best-selling books and is a media figure, a darling of the powerful American right. Early on it looked as if his career as a Marine and a National Security Council aide would forever be linked to the shredding of documents by his secretary, Fawn Hall. Just a couple of years ago, an article on the renewed popularity of document shredders had the obligatory reference to "Ollie North and his bombshell secretary." The imagery verged on the farcical.

But North's role in the Iran-contra scandal—sending weapons to Iran in exchange for cat's-paw maneuvers to free American hostages elsewhere in the Middle East, with money diverted to the anti-Communist contra rebels in Nicaragua—was deadly serious.

The words of Federal District Judge Gerhard Gesell at North's sentencing say it best: "The indictment involves your participation in particular covert events. I do not think that in this area you were a leader at all, but really a low-ranking subordinate working to carry out initiatives of a few cynical superiors. You came to be the point man in a very complex power play developed by higher-ups. Whether it was because of the excitement and the challenge or because of conviction, you responded certainly willingly and sometimes even excessively to their requirements. And along the way you came to accept, it seems to me, the mistaken view that Congress couldn't be trusted and that the fate of the country was better left to a small inside group, not elected by the people, who were free to act as they chose while publicly professing to act differently. Thus you became and by a series of circumstances in fact and I believe in your mind part of a scheme that reflected a total distrust in some constitutional values."

Illustrations Credits

17, The Granger Collection; 18, Library of Congress (LC-USZ62-100476); 21, National Archives (148-GW-556); 24, Library of Congress (LC-DIG-cwpb-03855); 27, Library of Congress (LC-USZ62-109385); 31, Bettmann/CORBIS; 32, Ronald Siemoneit/CORBIS SYGMA; 37, Library of Congress (LC-USZ62-68483); 38, Hulton Archive/Getty Images; 41, Imagno/Getty Images; 42, Hulton Archive/Getty Images; 45, Topham/The Image Works; 48,Geoffrey Manasse/Time Life Pictures/Getty Images; 51, Bettmann/CORBIS; 53, Bettmann/CORBIS; 54, Jeffrey Markowitz/CORBIS SYGMA; 58, AP Photo/FBI; 61, AP Photo/FBI; 66, Bettmann/CORBIS; 69, AP/Wide World Photos; 70, The National Archives of the U.K.: ref. KV2/70; 73, Evening Standard/Getty Images; 75, Hulton Archive/Getty Images; 78, Bettmann/CORBIS; 84, Catherine Karnow/CORBIS; 87, Bettmann/CORBIS; 90, Michael Nicholson/CORBIS; 93, Bettmann/CORBIS; 94, Library of Congress (LC-DIG-cwpbh-03501); 96, AP/Wide World Photos; 99, National Archives; 100, CORBIS; 104, From the collection of Andrew Cook; 107, Mansell/Time Life Pictures/Getty Images; 109, National Archives (65-H-125-8); 113, Wally McNamee/CORBIS; 116, AP/Wide World Photos; 120, Topical Press Agency/Hulton Archive/Getty Images; 123, U.S. Government photograph; 124, Life Magazine/Time Life Pictures/Getty Images; 128, Hulton-Deutsch Collection/CORBIS; 130 & 133, Courtesy Antonio Mendez; 136, Michael Nicholson/CORBIS; 139, Library of Congress (LC-DIG-ppmsca-02909); 140, Bettmann/CORBIS; 143, Carl Van Vechten Photograph Collection, Library of Congress (LC-DIG-ppmsca-07816); 144, John Springer Collection/CORBIS; 148, Keystone/Getty Images; 151, Underwood & Underwood/CORBIS; 153, Library of Congress (LC-USZ62-101098); 154, Hulton Archive/Getty Images; 159, Peter Stackpole/Time Life Pictures/Getty Images; 160, Express Newspapers/Getty Images; 164, Evening Standard/Getty Images; 171, Slim Aarons/Getty Images; 173, Tony Linck/Time Life Pictures/Getty Images; 174, Nick Ut, AP/Wide World Photos; 179, U.S. Air Force photograph; 180, Sovfoto; 187, rgm/Auckland Star, AP/Wide World Photos; 188, Wally McNamee/CORBIS.

All illustrations by Steven Guarnaccia, except "Fingerprint" on page 2 and 192 and "No Photo on File" on page 83 and 184 by Melissa Farris.

I LIE FOR A LIVING:
Greatest Spies of All Time

Researched and Written by Antony Shugaar
Principal Consultant, Peter Earnest, Executive Director, International Spy Museum
Manuscript review by Dr. Thomas Boghardt, Historian, International Spy Museum

Published by the National Geographic Society
John M. Fahey, Jr., President and Chief Executive Officer
Gilbert M. Grosvenor, Chairman of the Board
Nina D. Hoffman, Executive Vice President; President, Books and School Publishing

Prepared by the Book Division
Kevin Mulroy, Senior Vice President and Publisher
Kristin Hanneman, Illustrations Director
Marianne R. Koszorus, Design Director

Staff for this Book
Lisa Lytton, Editor
Rebecca Lescaze, Text Editor
Melissa Farris, Art Director/Illustrations Editor
Meredith Wilcox, Editorial Illustrations Specialist
Kelton Higgins, Illustrations Research
Rebecca Hinds, Managing Editor
Gary Colbert, Production Director

Manufacturing and Quality Management
Christopher A. Liedel, Chief Financial Officer
Phillip L. Schlosser, Vice President
John T. Dunn, Technical Director
Vincent P. Ryan, Director
Chris Brown, Director
Maryclare Tracy, Manager

With special thanks to Milt and Tamar Maltz and Joan G. Stanley of J.G. Stanley & Co., Inc.

Visit the International Spy Museum, Washington, D.C. and spymuseum.org